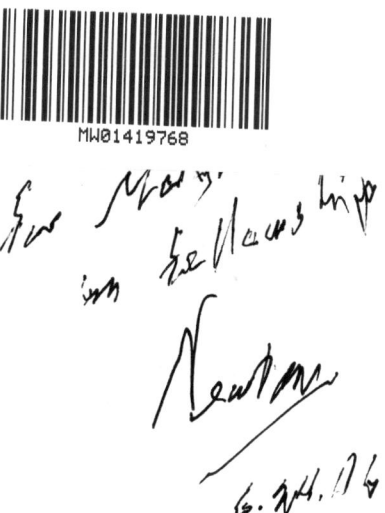

LIMITS TO POWER

Center Working Papers are works-in-progress, or edited texts of interviews, lectures and symposia presented by the Center for Studies in American Culture, a unit of the University at Buffalo, State University of New York.

Editorial Board

Howard S. Becker
Diane Christian
Robert Creeley†
David Felder
Bruce Jackson
John Mohawk

NEWTON GARVER

LIMITS TO POWER

SOME FRIENDLY REMINDERS

CENTER WORKING PAPERS

Limits to Power: Some Friendly Reminders © 2006 by Newton Garver. All rights reserved. Printed in the United States of America. No part of this book may be used or reproduced in any manner whatsoever without written permission except in the case of brief quotations in critical articles or reviews.

ISBN 0-931627-17-6

Center for Studies in American Culture
610 Capen Hall
University at Buffalo
Buffalo, New York 14269960
http://centerworkingpapers.com
csac@buffalo.edu

To the memory of Bayard Rustin, a radically left-handed friend.

A mediocre man who achieves what he intends is not the ideal of a free man. To be free is something like this: to exist sanely without fear and to perceive what is real.
—Iris Murdoch

CONTENTS

Preface ix

INVOCATION

God Bless America! 3

I: LEFT-HANDED ESSAYS

1. Shadow of the 60s 7
2. 9/11 Plus 30 11
3. Freedom and Accountability 17
4. The News and the Truth 20
5. The Politics of Humiliation 24
6. Idolatry 28

II: FOCUS ON BOLIVIA

7. Bolivia in Turmoil 39
8. Bolivia at a Crossroads 48
9. The Anti-political Politician 54
10. Bolivia: Preparing the Third Revolution 59
11. Roadblocks to Power 67

EPILOGUE

Heraclitus's Reply 79

Preface

David Brooks recently concluded that America is becoming more virtuous (*New York Times,* August 7, 2005). It is not a conclusion that appeals to a reflective Quaker. While one can agree that the reduction in crime, violence, and teen pregnancy is welcome news, and makes life easier for many, the larger picture remains that of a nation of arrogant, greedy, self-centered, and indifferent persons and policies. George Fox taught that our cheerfulness and salvation depend on our being patterns and examples for all those who are tempted by social conformity and political power. As I look upon our society with my Quaker eyes, it is with horror and disbelief that I note the behavior of Americans in the context of Fox's advice. Unrestrained spending on armament (more than the rest of the world combined) and on prisons (the world leader here, too), reduction of fuel efficiency through ever-larger and more powerful vehicles, expenditure of 14% to 15% of our GDP on health-care, 5000-square-foot mansions for small families, second homes that are grandiose but occupied only a few weeks in the year, recklessly increasing public and private debt—these and a host of other foibles are patterns and examples for alienation and disaster rather than for cheerfulness or salvation that come through fellowship—let alone for freedom or justice.

I can neither swim comfortably in this mainstream of indulgent hedonism and paranoid protectionism, nor find a way to swim out of it. A Quaker and a philosopher, and left-handed to boot, I work and breathe easily only at the edge—or at Eliot's "still center," when I can find it. I live a comfortable middle-class life and enjoy deep fellowship with many friends. Trying to live peaceably and constructively, I feel outrage at the sophomoric rationalizations for the brutality and indifference that accompany our reckless indulgence and our paranoid reliance on repression. Insofar as I believe at all in hell, I think this country is on the road to hell. I am deeply disaffected, even though I am not unhappy or discontent; I am uneasy in spite of the comfort of my living conditions.

I do not mean that I feel lonely in my disaffection. After all, George Fox, founder of the Quakers, was both beaten by mobs and thrown into prison by the authorities for his views, and Socrates was sentenced to death for his by a democratic vote in Athens. My modern companions include such colleagues at University at Buffalo as Bruce Jackson and Gerry Rising. Bruce has been vilified by "official" Jewish voices for publishing and defending criticisms of Israeli policy; and after Gerry wrote a column urging parents to defend science teachers in the schools, the many unhappy comments he received led him to write that "I feel increasingly that I am in a foreign land." So we are not lonely, those of us who are strangers in our own lands.

At times I am tempted just to scream, except that screaming would be infantile and easily overcome by the sophomoric rationalizations. Some alternative is required. The Inquisition relied on "Blasphemy!" and "Heresy!" Dickens preferred "Humbug!" Herman Schwartz made great use of "You can't be serious!" and Harry Frankfurt has brought "Bullshit!" out of the shadows. These all have their place. They focus attention and are certainly preferable to screaming. I use them all from time to time. But my preferred medium is the essay that takes a reader deeper into the rich concepts that frame our discourse and our dilemmas, and it has been a wonderful stimulation to have the *Buffalo Report* as a forum where these might be published.

In the collection that follows, I have called one section, "Left-handed Essays" to reflect my sense that David Brooks and George Will would consider my thoughts and reservations to be at least gauche if not sinister. My mother was not happy that I proved to have an inborn left-handedness, and for a time she tried to reform me by tying my preferred hand behind my back. She knew that left-handed is "sinister" in Latin and "gauche" in French, although she was probably unaware that the Quran groups the blessed on the right hand of Allah. Never altogether excluded, but on the margins of every society. The effect of mother's efforts, however, was not reform of my left-handedness but its reinforcement. It is now a point of pride, and these essays articulate some of its dimensions.

Our public discourse is dominated by politics, in the sense of a divisive and all-inclusive striving for control and domination by one's party and one's friends. Politics is intrinsically right-handed. In this context I have been exceedingly grateful that *Buffalo Report* has provided a forum through which I can express views that seem not to fit comfortably in the standard media. The Left-handed Essays all comment on the forum for public discourse and the distortions created by politicians, editors, and pundits. They are all critical of this status quo and sometimes of the Administration, but without in any case endorsing the "other" party. I have no wish to retract anything in them, but I might add further comments pertaining to the essay "Idolatry," which touches on an ancient and unending theme and resounds most poignantly today.

In the spring of 2005 there appeared a new book by Chris Hedges, *Losing Moses on the Freeway: the Ten Commandments in America*. Each chapter takes one of the commandments as its epigraph and then proceeds in a double fashion, first telling a story or two, from his own wide experience as a correspondent, and then ringing out accusations against our culture for abandoning, in the manner of these stories, the crux of the commandment. Idols are the explicit topic of the second commandment, but idolatry comes up again and again in the discussion of the others. Like me, Hedges gives a suggestive list of principal idols, not mentioning even one of my seven "P's": rock stars, nation, race, religion, ethnicity, gender, and class. I have no quarrel at all with this list, since no list can be complete. Every reader will be able to think of other idols. The key is noticing the difference between worship and practical rationality, for there is nothing practical about our behavior toward idols. Idolatry, unfortunately, is commonly a group phenomenon, and then it becomes vicious as well as stupefying, for the groups exercise control and domination by demanding conformity. This is generally true with the idolizing of nation-states and holy scriptures, from which I and my companions stand in greatest jeopardy today.

My left-handed antidote for idolatry is not atheism or wholesale scepticism but lively attention to the insight that conscience is the voice of God. Conscience seems a characteristically left-handed trait, regularly leaving one at odds with institutions and traditions.

Five of the essays are on Bolivia, which celebrated 180 years of Independence on August 6, 2005. For most of its independence, Bolivia had the most incompetent and the most repressive government in the hemisphere, or close to it. Until the second half of the 20th century, none of its governments was ever elected, its leaders were often generals, and they lost all five of the wars into which they led their nation. As a consequence, Bolivia now occupies only half of the territory it commanded at the time of independence, generous slices having been carved off by each of its neighbors. And today it ranks as the poorest country in South America with the possible exception of Guiana. So much for incompetence. Until 1950, it was understood that the sale of a hacienda included all the peasants living and working there. Indians were also worked to death in the mines whose products and profits left the country, and of course they had no access to either education or voting. The emancipation of Bolivian Indians (30,000 of whom are Quakers) did not occur until 1952 under the leadership of Victor Paz Estenssoro. So much for repression.

In the past few years the Bolivian Indians have developed and exercised power to stop government measures to which they are united in their opposition. Although still the poorest segment of the poorest nation, they have enough education, political savvy, and organization to compete seriously in upcoming elections. In the essays comprising the third section of this volume I have tried to describe the principal dynamics of the emerging development and maturation of indigenous political power in Bolivia. These essays are of course dated, but they may still provide a backdrop for what may prove to be an historic transition of political power to Amerindians.

The epilogue to this collection is the only piece not written within the past three years. It was written in 1980 as a reaction to a powerful remark from Joseph Conrad's novel *Victory*: "I only know that he who forms a tie is lost. The germ of corruption has entered his soul."

I came across this passage as the epigraph to Graham Greene's novel *The Human Factor*. Greene's novel develops a scenario involving a double agent for whom Conrad's remark is true, in the sense that the hero loses his life because of an emotional relationship. I find Conrad's remark haunting because it is as impossible to take it as wholly true as it is to reject it as wholly false.

Beyond this enigmatic feature of Conrad's remark, there is also the beginning phrase "I only know…". I am inveterately suspicious of knowledge claims, and doubly so when they are combined with some sort of exclusivity. I take science to provide our paradigm for knowledge, and exclusivity of any kind is anathema for scientific knowledge. So I regarded Conrad's first three words as outrageous, although I also recognize them as the sort of thing many ordinary people might say.

When I wrote *Heraclitus's Reply* I wanted to express my outrage, which I then thought would be impossible in my ordinary essay style. So I wrote it in the form of a poem, using some of the devices (such as excessive and half-hidden erudition), and some lines, of T.S. Eliot. The first part of the poem addresses the unsettling exclusiveness attributed to the knowledge claim, the second part addresses the paradox of *saying* that he who forms a tie is lost, and the third part invokes Heraclitus as a basis for responding to the haunting claim of the speaker. The first part is both playful (with a trilingual pun at one point) and pseudo-philosophical. One line ("This gift is plainly an illusion") is a direct quotation from F. H. Bradley's *Appearance and Reality*, and is philosophically cogent as well. There are also mischievous borrowings from Quine, Wittgenstein, and Sartre. The third part of the poem articulates the response of Heraclitus to Conrad's main point: a thrust by one word miser's aphorism against the haunting half-truth of another. Here there are obvious borrowings from Dante and the New Testament as well as from Heraclitus and Eliot.

The whole poem has a tendentious quality inspired by the hidden intellectual depth of much of Eliot's work, but it lacks the poetic quality of that work. A poet once read over my work and remarked that it contained one good line ("the April bullet on a Memphis afternoon"). I would not attempt to write such a thing today, preferring straightforward prose, even for expressing outrage. I still believe that the main points of this poem are sound and deserve repeating, and today I can see the form that such an essay might take. On the one hand it would make use of Iris Murdoch's critique of romantic individualism, which is a useful label for Conrad's standpoint as well as for the notion of special or exclusive knowing. On the other hand it would make use of David Stern's recent introduction of Wittgenstein's *Investigations* (Cambridge 2005) to show

how Greene's exploration of conditions for the truth of the passage parallels Wittgenstein's use of language-games in the early sections of his later work. Stern points out that when Wittgenstein brings forth from Augustine (*Investigations* §1) or from Plato (*Investigations* §46) a resounding philosophical claim that needs deflating, the second stage in his work of clarification is to construct a concrete situation in which the remark holds true. The third stage, which Stern notes is sometimes implicit rather than explicit, is then to show how limited the situation is and how dependent on various tacit understandings. One might then take Greene's novel as the second stage of a Wittgensteinian treatment of Conrad's romantic temptation. But I leave that essay for another occasion.

In posting these pieces on Buffaloreport.com, I never anticipated that they would appear in a volume. The volume is a working paper, befitting the title of the series in which it appears. It is only in such a series that the four parts could go together. I am grateful to Bruce Jackson for suggesting that they be published together, as well as for his efforts to give my thoughts a wider airing. At a time when the media is so dominated by such a stifling atmosphere, it is refreshing as well as valuable to have alternative options such as those provided by *Buffalo Report* and the Center Working Papers.

East Concord NY— September 7, 2005

Invocation

God Bless America!

Many bumper stickers ask that God bless America. I have thought a lot about what it would mean, and what hopes attend the bumper stickers. I can't really bring myself to believe that God chooses sides in politics or wars any more than in basketball games, so I doubt God's blessings would be what everybody expects or hopes.

In the Old Testament God does take sides in battles, for example on behalf of David and Hezekiah. But this partisan favor never comes easily, and it never seems to protect the rich and powerful. Lots of people who ask for help get kicked in the head instead. A precondition is always repenting of having forsaken God for worldly wealth and power. Powerful people don't fare very well, and arrogance leads to disaster. Think of Goliath and Sennacherib. Isn't America more like Goliath than like David?

In the New Testament the good news is a Gospel of Peace, promised by a God of Love. The teaching is to live in a manner that takes away the occasion for war, which no modern politicians take as a serious option at all. I wonder if even David could have mustered Gospel support for his fight against Goliath. Wealth does not absolutely preclude blessings, but it sure gets in the way. Peace and love are the blessings promised by the Gospel, and they would be welcome blessings indeed.

Humility (or repentance) is required for God's blessings -- an acknowledgment of falling short, growing fat and lazy, taking too much for granted. I will suppose that each reader can best do this privately, as I do, including thanks for what we already have, so I will proceed directly to ask for God's blessings, as I understand them.

Dear God, bless us with your Spirit of Love, that we may through our words and deeds awaken that same Spirit of Love and Charity which we know lies in the soul of every person. Let the miracles of love break down ancient enmities and overcome ugly rumors and suspicions.

Bless us with your Spirit of Truth, that we may tear away the masks of pretense and theory and speculation, which now gloss reality with false faces in the minds and utterances of our media, our neighbors, our leaders, and ourselves.

Bless us with your Spirit of Peace, that we may bring calm where there is panic, patience where there is urgency, and hope where there is fear. Protect us from the incessant demands of those who are hurried or worried, and bring them, too, to a calming acceptance of setbacks, failures, unwelcome facts, and losses.

Bless us with your Spirit of Hope, that we may sketch alternatives to gloomy forecasts and dire predictions, and may bring fuller attention to opportunities for reconciliation and growth that always accompany conflict and danger. Let hope rather than fear be the shadow that the future casts across our present lives.

Bless us with your Spirit of Joy, that we may keep your presence shining in our faces, that our spirits may rebuke the glumness and foreboding of the news of the day, and that we may sing and rejoice, knowing the work of the Lord.

Bless us with your Spirit of Light, that our eyes may see and our ears may hear, and that we may shine upon the hill and be a candle to the darkness and a voice in the wilderness.

God bless America!—May these blessings fall upon us and our leaders, and on the rest of the world, too, so we may all learn to find security in a spirit of peace and community, of truth and reconciliation, rather than in force of arms.

(December 25, 2003)

I: Left-Handed Essays

1   Shadows of the 60's

It is 35 years since the publication in *The Nation* of my essay "What Violence Is." The 60's were years of violence. In 1963 President Kennedy was assassinated. The next summer urban centers began erupting, with riots in Harlem when an off-duty police officer shot and killed a black youth. More riots (often with a similar spark) erupted in other cities (including Buffalo) during that and subsequent summers. Among the more serious were those in Newark and in the Watts district of Los Angeles. Rioting continued through 1967, when the worst occurred in Detroit. In April of 1968, in Memphis, Martin Luther King, Jr., was murdered. So the time was ripe for a thoughtful essay on what violence is.

I noted that President Johnson went on national television, on prime time, twice during that decade, in 1964 and 1968, urging the American people to realize that nothing can be achieved by violence. He was very eloquent, but it was hard not to notice a certain irony about his presenting this message just as he was escalating military activity in Vietnam. So is war not an instance of violence?—Well, not if you conceive of violence as the illegitimate use of force, which is just how John Dewey defined it.

A great deal can be said in defense of this Deweyan conception. The concept of violence is indeed complex, involving both a factual dimension having to do with force or coercion and a moral dimension having to do with legitimacy. But there are two big problems with the Dewey-Johnson version. One is that this definition lets the powers and principalities of the world off the hook far too easily, for they have legitimate authority on their side even when justice is not. The other is that this narrow definition of violence gives us no purchase on the concept of nonviolence as employed by Gandhi and King.

So I proposed that violence in human affairs (we want to leave aside violent storms) has more to do with violation than with force, and that humans can be violated in different ways. The violation can be either personal or institutional, and it can be either overt (using physical force) or covert or quiet (using psychology or social conventions). Rape, mugging, and murder are paradigms of overt personal violence. In war (and riots) on the other hand, the violation is overt but the victims are not targeted personally, and the perpetrators can rarely be said to have acted on their own personal initiative and responsibility. And so on, with examples and citations.

The essay ended: "The institutional form of quiet violence operates when people are deprived of choices in a systematic way by the very manner in which transactions normally take place. It is as real, and as wicked, as the thief with a knife."—Even today that sounds right.

The aftermath of the publication included two events worth pondering. On the final day of the Detroit riot, President Lyndon Johnson had appointed a special commission, widely known as the Kerner Commission, to investigate the civil disorders. In its report, delivered in 1968 shortly after the publication of my essay, the Commission identified institutional racism as an underlying cause of the rioting. Although this conclusion does not endorse any particular conception of violence, it certainly vindicates one of my principal contentions, namely that it makes little sense to deplore physical violations of property while ignoring institutional violations of persons.

The other event was more of a surprise. My essay was widely reprinted (to the benefit of *The Nation*, not me) and used to start discussions in university classes. Some three years later one of my colleagues in the Philosophy Department got a phone call from an instructor in San Francisco whose class had just read and discussed the article. The instructor wanted to know whether it is true, as the class had surmised, that Garver is a black nationalist!—What a wake-up call for this white pacifist! Who am I, anyway? Do I get to say? Or do other people define me, willy-nilly?

So on to today.

Today the buzz word is terrorism rather than violence, but some of the issues are the same. For the authorities of the day, as for Lyndon Johnson, nothing that is done by a half-way legitimate government could constitute either violence or terrorism. All the politicians and all the mainstream media work with a definition of terrorism parallel to Dewey's definition of violence, one that lets the authorities off the hook far too easily. It is as absurd to think that the "shock and awe" bombing of Bagdad was not designed to terrorize Iraqis as to think that the military action in Vietnam was not a kind of violence. The Pentagon was counting on the effects of terror working to the US advantage, just as Osama bin Laden counts on the effects of terror working to al Qaeda's advantage. Why should only the latter terror count as "terrorism"?

Another common denominator between then and now is the assumption that terrorism, like violence, is absolutely unjustifiable. That is fine for a pacifist like me, for whom violence is never justified. But Hannah Arendt has a more reasonable rule for the non-pacifists who constitute the vast majority—that those who commit acts of violence have the burden of proof: there is a moral presumption against them, but not yet a verdict of guilt. The same holds for terrorism, as was argued years ago, very persuasively, by Virginia Held in her paper "Terrorism, Rights, and Political Goals," which she read at UB in March 1989. Held considers herself an advocate of nonviolence, but she argues that those whose rights are being violated cannot be condemned for using whatever means may be necessary to achieve political goals that will end the violations of their rights, or at least render the rights-violations more equally distributed.

The official response to recent terrorism echoes the official response to the urban violence of the 60's, except that should not expect the appointment of anything like the Kerner Commission. The response is one of attempting to achieve domination and control by means of brute force, having no dialogue with the "enemy." A local example of such is the draconian prison sentences given to the Lackawanna Six, the six young citizens of Yemeni extraction who accepted free trips to Pakistan and Afghanistan—combined with no attempt at all to integrate these men and their families into US (or Erie County) society. A response of missed opportunities, typical of mainline politics. Crises always present opportunities to achieve wider unities through integration with adversaries or "others" by means of discourse and negotiation. Of course negotiation risks losing control. In fact it consists of losing control, or rather of renouncing control or domination by any one of the contending parties. The government chose to flex its muscle and show the Lackawanna Six who's in charge. Violence, terrorism, prisons, and armies are instruments for achieving domination and control. Discourse and negotiation involve working with rather than against the others, "them"; and that is risky. There are risks and opportunities everywhere. We are nudged away from the opportunities by being persuaded (deceived into thinking) that the risks are too great, far greater than we realize because of "the domino effect" or because of WMD that "we know" they have. Thus it is not conscience but paranoia that doth make cowards of us all.

We are told that the world changed completely on 9/11, but a great deal seems just the same as in 1968. In particular, politicians continue to thrive on paranoia, which requires none of the toughness, clarity, and courage that conscience demands.

NOTE: Held's paper can be found in *Justice, Law, and Violence* (ed. James B. Brady and Newton Garver, 1991). For those who have forgotten the taste of the violence of the 60's two excellent accounts are Robert E. Conot's *Rivers of Blood, Years of Darkness: The Unforgettable Classic Account of the Watts Riot* (1968) and John Hersey's *The Algiers Motel Incident* (1968).

(10 May 2003)

2 9/11 Plus 30

9/11 is a curious date, significant for bloody events on three continents. September 11, 2003, marks the 30th anniversary of the overthrow of the democratically elected government of Chile and the death of its President, Salvador Allende. On the same date in 1974 there was another bloody coup, this time in Africa where the government of Ethiopia was overthrown. Two years ago a strange twist of fate gave us another reason to remember 9/11. For most people in the USA the date is remembered only for the year 2001, not for 1973, certainly not for 1974. For most people in Chile, of course, 1973 and the thousands of murders and harsh brutalities of the ensuing years constitute an ongoing trauma.

9/11/73 differs from 9/11/01 in many ways, though both reflect aspects of who we are as a people. 9/11/73 was not, for us, a time when we knew that we were involved in the event of the day, and the trauma of the event stretched out over decades. 9/11/01 was an event which we all knew about immediately, and the trauma was intensified by being packed into a very short time-span. Thirty years later we know that roughly as many people were killed as a direct result of both events, but that knowledge, as our knowledge of our involvement and responsibility, was slow to emerge.

THE BACKGROUND

Salvador Allende was a Socialist, who had run unsuccessfully for the office in 1958 and 1964, efforts that were "probably foiled by the large sums of money that the USA—alarmed at the thought of a leftist government in Chile as well as Cuba—poured into their opponents' coffers," according to Dame Margaret Anstee, former Undersecretary General of the UN, in her useful book, *Never Learn to Type* (p. 294). In 1970 Allende won a plurality of 36.3 percent of the vote, and the election itself was put into the hands of the Chilean Congress. Anstee quotes former US Ambassador to Chile Nathaniel Davis as reporting that "President Nixon instructed the CIA to 'save Chile' from Allende (whom he referred to as 'that sonofabitch'), to 'leave no stone unturned. ... .to block Allende's confirmation' and to 'make the economy scream'" (p. 294). The CIA tricks backfired, and Allende was confirmed as President on November 24, 1970.

The economic pressure on Chile worked more slowly but more effectively. US economic aid was, of course, cut off, and the copper mines were nationalized, creating further friction with the Nixon administration. It must have been annoying to Nixon that the first year of Allende's government went well in spite of the pressures. Toward the end of 1971, however, inflation began to rise and the price of copper, Chile's main export, began to decline. Nathaniel Davis, in his book *The Last Two Years of Salvador Allende*, conjectures (pp. 21-22) that this may well have been the result of National Security Decision Memorandum 93 issued by Henry Kissinger in November 1970, which established a policy of pressure on Allende's government to prevent its consolidation and ordered a review of steps to drive down the price of copper.

The economy began to scream in 1972, and tensions with the US were exacerbated when issues about land reform were added to the issues about nationalization of the mines. Allende's image was not improved when Fidel Castro came for a ten-day visit and stayed three weeks. In October a crisis came in the form of a truckers' strike, which paralyzed the country and quickly spread to other sectors. Margaret Anstee gives reasons to think that the strike was financed from the US: "Now, in the midst of this nationwide strike, the Chilean peso, which had been dropping like a stone, suddenly rose in value, a highly unlikely phenomenon unless dollars were pouring in to support the strikers" (p. 302).

Meanwhile in Washington, there were several mysterious break-ins into the Chilean embassy in April and May of 1972. Who could have done that?

Coup and Consequences

The truckers' strike had inaugurated what Margaret Anstee saw as the beginning of a by then inevitable collapse of the government. On August 9, five weeks before the coup, she invited to dinner several ambassadors and several governmental ministers. The Chileans were unable, at the last moment, to come, but Anstee had a chance to size up the top US diplomat on the scene. She writes: "I was impressed with Nathaniel Davis's even-handed approach. The US was painted as the villain of the piece by Allende supporters, and there could be no doubt, as was amply proved later, that powerful US forces had long been at work to bring Allende down. My instinct at that dinner was that Davis, a career diplomat, was not a party to all this, and his book on Chile shows that he did not know the whole truth" (p. 313)

It is useful to be reminded that the US was not, and is not, monolithic.

Anstee was in New York at the time of the coup, but she returned to Chile as soon as she could, because of dangers not only to UN personnel but also to opponents of other Latin American military dictatorships who had taken refuge in Chile. "It is hard to convey the trauma of those days, the like of which I had never experienced before. It was an intolerable burden to know that the fate of human lives in some way rested in my hands," she writes (p. 326). September is the beginning of spring (rather than fall) in Chile, and the bursting blooms underscored nature's indifference to suffering: "The spring seemed heart-breakingly callous, early mists giving way to airy, sunny days in which the enchantment of my garden shone to its best effect—clusters of purple and white violets, banks of azaleas and rhododendrons tumbling down to the river, bright camellias glowing in the dark shade of eucalyptus groves. The contrast with the grisly events of the day.—corpses floating down the lower reaches of the same River Mapocho, as I drove to the office, and countless scenes of human misery—was unbearable" (p. 327).

Corpses floating down the river is a particularly graphic image. General Pinochet seems to have shared Richard Nixon's unforgiving animosity toward opponents, which included nearly all those who had worked with Allende or been sympathetic to him. There were thousands of executions over the years. Even those who managed to be out of the country were not safe. General Prats, head of the army and Interior Minister under Allende, was murdered along with his wife in Buenos Aires in September 1974. Orlando Letelier, Allende's Foreign Minister, was blown up by a car bomb in Washington, D.C., in 1976—a crime that remains unsolved, leading some to wonder whether the CIA's involvement with Pinochet may have impeded the investigation.

Who Are We?—Who Am I?

We all have things in our past that we do not include in our résumés. Some sense of shame and embarrassment is natural and innocent, but blindness and denial are not. There were indeed other factors at work in the overthrow of Allende's government. He was under pressure from the right (the Christian Democrats) for doing anything at all to advance the platform of his party, and under equal pressure from the more radical wing of his party to move faster and with more sweeping action. It was a tenuous balance, and it was no doubt because of the precariousness of the balance that the US dirty tricks worked so well. But dirty tricks there were, and they were ours. We are not just the people who suffered the trauma of 9/11/01 but also the people who fostered and unleashed the decades of trauma in Chile that began with 9/11/73. Terror as well as trauma.

Nixon was our President, and he was on a crusade—he was not afraid to call it that—against communism, and everyone who was not with "us" in that crusade was against us. Bush is cut from Nixon cloth, but tailored differently, so the sanctimonious blandness replaces Nixon's vulgarity. Instead of a "crusade against communism" it is a "war against terrorism." As early as September 14, 2001, in his declaration of war at the National Cathedral, Bush declared that any country not supporting us in this effort would be regarded as giving aid and comfort to terrorism, and hence as an enemy. This is not the place to catalog all the places where we are instigators of terror and trauma in the present world, but it would be blindness or denial to fail to acknowledge that that was our role in Chile thirty years ago. It is part of who we are.

We sometimes undermine democracy. That is part of who we are, alas. 9/11/73 was a subversion of democracy, abetted by us (through Nixon) as part of our crusade against communism. Then, as today, we may be told that the crusade is really a crusade for democracy and freedom. But crusades by their very nature are incompatible with democracy and freedom. As Chile and Pinochet ought to teach us, they are characterized by too much intolerance and brutality for that.

Lest We Forget

A modest proposal. I am all for remembering our sufferings and our achievements, but cannot agree that they should erase remembrance of our faults. 9/11 is a momentous date partly because it commemorates us both as instigators and as victims of terror and trauma. We are now building a monument to 9/11 at the World Trade Center site in Manhattan. So let us arrange for a small plaque somewhere in the new plaza remembering the tragedy of 9/11/73—a simple plaque, without the thousands of names of victims, and perhaps without even an explicit acknowledgment of our role in the affair. Just something to show that ours is not the only suffering the world has seen on 9/11. Perhaps even a note about 9/11/74. It would by no means atone for the suffering we caused, nor even acknowledge it, but it would be one small welcome step.

(10 May 2003)

3   Freedom and Accountability

Paul Krugman's column in the *New York Times* of June 10, 2003, "Who's Accountable?", scratches the surface of a deep problem. Krugman notes that the Administration has attacked those criticizing the slipshod arguments for the war in Iraq, the "cherry-picking" of slim favorable evidence and suppression of solid grounds for doubts about WMD, the wholly fabricated implication that Saddam supported the network of Osama bin Laden and was therefore involved in the attacks on the World Trade Center and the Pentagon. Krugman is with the critics. And it is not just an intellectual game, since these shoddy rationalizations led the US into war, and the costs of the war were in the process vastly underestimated. Two years later the public is increasingly accepting the view that the Administration misled the nation by manipulating intelligence reports and dressing up news releases. Krugman's question is why no one is being held accountable for these very costly misjudgments, and his point is that sound vibrant government depends on officials being held accountable for deceptions and other frauds as well as for crimes and corrupt practices. Bravo! He is right that our liberty depends in this way on accountability, which is sorely lacking the politics of the day. Two cheers for this insight.

   I say that he scratches the surface because there is a deeper issue about freedom and accountability, one that is more unsettling than the problem about holding the malefactors responsible. The problem is what it means to be free and autonomous. There is superficial sense of freedom in which I am free if I am unimpeded. It sounds wonderful, but thought through it collapses. To be free and autonomous means to be able to fend for yourself in the real world, where freedom and consequences are inseparable not just morally but also ontologically. In spite of their abstractions and their metaphors, it is useful to keep "heavies" like Wittgenstein and Sartre in mind when thinking of these matters.

In the *Philosophical Investigations* (#107) Wittgenstein says: "We have got on to slippery ice where there is no friction and so in a certain sense the conditions are ideal, but also, just because of that, we are unable to walk. We want to walk: so we need *friction*. Back to the rough ground!" Wittgenstein never wrote about politics, but being able to act so that you never have to face the consequences seems just like being on the slippery ice where "in a certain sense the conditions are ideal." The instances of slippery ice that Krugman mentions could easily be multiplied, for political ideology of all sorts is designed for the very purpose of smoothing over the rough ground so that the violence and deception of governments and officials become frictionless actions. Quite apart from the moral questions Krugman rightly raises, there is also the more profound question whether there is really any genuine autonomy so divorced from the frictions of the real world. I don't want to forget the moral issue, but it would be a shame to let moralism altogether obscure this deeper ontological question.

Sartre's contribution to these matters are found brilliantly presented in his play *The Condemned of Altona*. The play concerns a family (modeled on the Krupps) living in Altona, a rich suburb of Hamburg. Prior to WWII the elder son, letting compassion overrule prudence, brings home a Jew to give him refuge. The matter is uncovered, the Jew is captured and killed, and the son suffers no consequences, shielded by his powerful father. But conscience is another matter, and the son anguishes with guilt. He tries to assuage this guilt by joining the Luftwaffe and flying suicidal missions, but ironically ends up with a medal for distinguished military service, a public confirmation of the allegiance he privately wishes to disavow. So he is a Nazi willy-nilly. After the war he assaults an American officer who has been deriding Nazis, saying that he is a Nazi—and is once again shielded from consequences by his powerful parent. From then on he lives sequestered in an inner room of the mansion, speaking only with his sister, until years later he finally emerges and drives himself and his father off a high bridge to their death.

Such encapsulation does scant justice to Sartre, all of whose work approaches over and again, from various angles, how it is possible to be a free and responsible human being. One of his lessons is that without accountability there is no freedom, that being shielded from consequences leads to sequestration rather than freedom. Looked at in this perspective, the facts that Krugman recounts do not generate moralistic outrage so much as sadness and despair at the illusions and missed opportunities.

Krugman, assisted by Wittgenstein and Sartre, leads me to ask whether we are not perhaps babying our soldiers and politicians. Sound parenting requires guarding infants from dangers of the harsh world, but such protection must cease if maturity and character are to emerge. A pernicious paternalism (or maternalism) is the consequence of overextending parental protection—of babying adolescents and adults—and it is this pernicious paternalism that I understand Sartre's play to be dissecting. It is difficult to believe that it is less pernicious in politics than in parenting.

(10 May 2003)

4 The news and the truth

Professional Ethics vs. Morals

Press ethics is one part of public institutional ethics, that is, the rules that apply to the professions and to public offices. With regard to any special area there are bound to be some minor differences, but the large issues are similar. We depend on professionals and office-holders for responsible decisions and responsible opinions, and the ethical issues therefore aim both at achieving such results and at showing or certifying responsibility in these matters.

Professional and political ethics differs sharply from morals in that professionals and politicians generally formulate their codes of ethics so as to permit lying and other deception that contravenes ordinary morality. The argument is that professional duties, or duties of office, or the exigencies of the situation, preclude ordinary truth-telling. Thus lawyers must put forth the best case for their clients, doctors must avoid truths that will depress or discourage their patients, Senator McCarthy and the President must protect their sources, and so on. The justification for lies and other deceptions takes the same form as the justifications for violence: "Sorry, but they are necessary—and they are legitimate because we are legitimate. So you better find another word—say, 'force' rather than 'violence' and 'spin' rather than 'lie'."

As a consequence of this professionalization of "ethics" most of the role-models in public life present models of "legitimate" lying and deceiving, just as governmental leaders provide models of force and threats of force as a "legitimate" way to solve problems. Professional and public necessities supposedly require this deviation from common morality. Some form of the Golden Rule is universal as a test of common morality, and these elements of professional and governmental ethics regularly fail—no professional or office-holder would agree to be deceived or coerced in the manner in which they deceive and coerce others.

Morality is undermined everywhere by such role models. Ordinary people invent their own "necessities" to match the invented "necessities" of professionals and office-holders, and the clash fills the prisons.

The boundaries and limits of this process are, of course, constantly being tested. Scandals in the past few years have shown that the public will not tolerate accountants putting the best face on their clients' books to the same extent that we expect both prosecuting and defense attorneys to present their best case, truth be damned. On the other hand the extent of deception that is tolerated from the White House under the rubrics of "spin" and "vulnerable sources" seems to have grown considerably. Because of the tension between professional/institutional ethics and morality, we can expect the boundaries to remain unstable.

TRUTH-TELLING.

Truth-telling is recognized as an ordinary virtue in every field of human endeavor, and it is this virtue that has special relevance to the press. Telling the truth involves at least three distinct matters, relevance, accuracy and sincerity. Relevance is breached, and our trust in the speaker is undermined, by lengthy stories, possibly accurate to the last detail, that are of only marginal relevance to the issue at hand – "human interest" stories are probably the most prevalent form of irrelevance in the press. Accuracy is breached, and our trust in it is undermined, by vagueness as well as by errors. Sincerity is breached, and our trust in it is undermined, by lies and deception. Max Black may have exaggerated when he said that politicians are inveterate liars, but it is certainly true that our leaders and role models regularly and unblushingly engage in irrelevance, inaccuracy and deception.

A great deal, so far as clear thinking is concerned, hangs on how "spinning" stands in relation to lying. Three comments. First, legally there is all the difference in the world, as there should be. Even though both spinning and lying are attempts to deceive, only lying involves saying what you know, or ought to know, to be straightforwardly false. It is appropriate that this more egregious form of deception be subject to legal penalties. Second, politicians exploit this legalism shamelessly. In politics it is not appropriate, and they deserve to be slapped down for it—which the press has generally failed to do. Third, morally there is no significant difference between spins and lies. It is the attempt to deceive that is morally relevant, since that in itself, whatever form it takes, violates the Golden Rule.

THE PRESS ON TRIAL.

The recent press scandals are a tempest in a teapot. Frauds occur everywhere. They need to be dealt with, but unless they are widespread, as in accounting, they are a merely local phenomenon. The two recent cases involved breaches of sincerity as well as accuracy, and such breaches seem rare. Current shortcomings of the press have to do with other matters – other breaches of relevance, accuracy, and sincerity.

Breaches of relevance seem the most serious of the shortcomings, and also the most difficult to describe and assess. It is often difficult to know what the issue really is; discerning real issues from pseudo issues is one of the principal and most difficult tasks of an editor. It is nevertheless clear that human interest stories, which dominate much of the press, have primarily an entertainment rather than a news value. For example, giving prominence to the rescue of Jessica Lynch, even if it had been accurate, was a breach of duties of relevance with respect to the news. Matters of some relevance that have been under-noticed include that Iraq has been a secular rather than Islamic state, that Saddam cracked down hard on Islamic militants, and that women held high office in Iraq. Failure to discern the relevance of such matters is a breach of relevance that can be charged to the press, and that helps explain the widespread public belief—utterly false—that Saddam was tied to al-Qaeda and shared responsibility for 9/11. Such widespread misconceptions on public issues constitute a far greater scandal for the press than the two recent frauds.

Breaches of accuracy seem most commonly to involve accepting spin as fact. For example, if the issue is whether Iraq has WMD, a statement by the President that he "knows" that Iraq has WMD cannot be accepted as establishing the fact. In this case what the President said was probably a bare-faced lie—he must have known that his evidence was fallible and that his belief fell short of knowledge. The press often follows a report with the warning, "The report has not been independently confirmed," but this is never done in the case of obviously self-serving statements from the White

House. The press thereby becomes complicit in the deception perpetrated by the political spin. Again, this sort of breach seems to me far more serious than the inventions of two bad apples.

Breaches of sincerity on the part of the press generally involve editorializing the news. Recently ownership of the media has become more concentrated, with the prospect that the owners will insist on having editors with a corporate and Republican bias, and will further insist on editorializing the news. Perhaps; but it is noteworthy that for decades the Wall Street Journal has kept its very right-wing editorial view separate from its coverage of the news. More apparent has been the recent beating of the war drums in the news columns, as if deviation from the Administration's foreign policy were a sort of treason. The press generally has wanted to support the war effort, and in the course of its enthusiasm has presented propaganda as fact, conniving in a deception of the public.

Every aspect of public morality is problematic, because of the tension between professional ethics and common morality. The press is certainly partly responsible for the high degree of public misinformation about Iraq and the UN, but does not deserve the beatings they have been taking because of the recent scandals. Lies and spins are both deceptions, and therefore both are contrary to the Golden Rule.

The large unnoticed problem, from a moral point of view, is that the highest office-holders model immorality—deception and violence—in the guise of privileged necessities. The press has succumbed to these seductive role-models, but no more than other professions.

(10 May 2003)

5   The Politics of Humiliation

Revelation of the humiliation of Iraqi prisoners at Abu Ghraib caught the world off guard, and expressions of outrage have been clamorous. Such treatment of fellow human beings is an outrage and deserves to be condemned. But I confess to being surprised and a little puzzled by the clamor and surprise. Except for the details and the photos, Abu Ghraib was, after all, a natural consequence of the politics of humiliation combined with the iron curtain of secrecy. The magnitude of the public reaction suggests that most people lack an understanding of the politics of humiliation.

POLITICS

Part of the politics of humiliation is politics that is both hard-headed and hard hearted. Such politics is about power, not about welfare. In one of the most powerful essays of the twentieth century, *Der Begriff des Politischen* (*The Concept of the Political*, 1932), Carl Schmitt insisted that politics is grounded in an arbitrary distinction between friends and foes. Friends are people or states prepared to fight (or campaign) with you: a coalition of the willing. Foes are those who go onto something like Nixon's famous "enemies list": they are those against whom you are prepared to fight (or campaign). Politics in this sense cannot exist without enemies; there must be at least two opposed parties or nation-states.

Schmitt argued that the division between friends and foes is arbitrary and ultimate. It is arbitrary in that it is not based on any issue or rational criterion. If there is an issue, it can in principle be resolved by some combination of lawyers, bankers, scientists, and diplomats, and then politics has no role to play. What happened at Pugwash is that the agreement of Hans Bethe and Andrei Sakharov about the detectability of nuclear tests made the politicians irrelevant: the Cold War went into temporary eclipse. The division is absolute in that the parties are prepared to go to war. Schmitt quotes with approval the famous remark of

Clausewitz that war is a continuation of politics by other means—which shows what kind of thing they think that politics is.

Schmitt was adamant that politics has nothing to do with morality, and that the distinction between friend and foe cannot be grounded in morality. It is a matter of us against them, not of good against evil. Both sides are human, so a politician who characterizes "them" as morally inferior risks not only the hubris of arrogance but also the blasphemy of denying God to be the creator of all.

Schmitt believed that politics properly belongs to nation-states, since they alone have the power to make war. This is a reasonable position. Nonetheless, partisan politics, particularly electoral politics in the USA today, involves a similar dichotomy between "us" and "them," with the proportions of rich and not-so-rich, as well as of virtue and cunning, roughly the same on both sides of the line. What is at stake is power, not righteousness—and not problem-solving.

Government, of course, requires paying some attention to problem-solving. There are alternative conceptions of politics—those of Aristotle and Rawls, for example—that regard politics as the art of government rather than the pursuit of power. Politicians often implement that conception when they act as legislators. But it is Schmitt's conception that takes center stage when someone says, "The people are tired of politics; they want us to put politics aside and get down to the business of government." Or again, when we speak of the politics of humiliation.

Humiliation

Humiliation is not a proper part of politics in either Schmitt's conception or in alternative conceptions. Humiliation is both a kind of action and a feeling that often accompanies the action and is always meant to accompany it. The action is one that deliberately treats a person as having a status inferior to the actual status of the person or to the status that the person deserves or previously enjoyed. The status being denied may be a common one that involved no ceremony, as when an adult is treated as a child, or it may be a special status, as when a soldier is given a dishonorable discharge or when a parishioner is excommunicated.

Schmitt mixed religion with his tough conception of politics. He was a right-wing Catholic, believing that the power of the Lord was over all, even over one's enemies. From his perspective it would be blasphemy to treat one's foes as less than human. We are all moral equals, on this view, even though politics sometimes makes it "necessary" to kill one's enemies. Religion, however, often gets mixed with politics in a different—and to my mind less honorable—way, whereby "we" become identified as the Lord's agents on this beleaguered earth, and "they" are identified as evil. Such sanctimonious arrogance is widespread; and though it is particularly virulent among the neocons and their supporters in the Bible Belt, it also lives in the opening lines of one of Rilke's sonnets:

What will you do, God, when I die,
When I, your pitcher, broken lie?

The Rest of the Iceberg

Abu Ghraib is horrible and disgusting, but it is not the main thing. The popular adage might be that Abu Ghraib is just the tip of the iceberg. And the VP uttering an obscenity at Senator Leahy was another, smaller, part of the tip. That is not a bad beginning at getting things in proper proportion. Beneath these newsworthy incidents lies a whole culture that disdains its opponents and critics and is quick to belittle them at any turn. The iceberg includes the Rush Limbaughs and Charles Krauthammers, and even the NY Times, when it editorializes that the peasants who threw out Bolivian President Gonzales Sanchez need to overcome their "nationalism and economic ignorance." We are plagued with a politics of humiliation that begins with disdain and verbal put-downs.

Arrogance, whether based on religion or ideology, has little use for knowledge and experience. What need is there for the accumulated wisdom of civilization when one is directly inspired and guided by God or by abstract theory? So the Bush administration has cast aside with disdain both experts and expertise —Hans Blix, Paul O'Neill, Richard Clarke, a whole cadre of diplomats, another cadre of generals, the French experience in Algeria, Arab scholars such as Walid and Rashid Khaladi, and so on. In each case there is a pooh-poohing that attempts to lower their status. In other words, disdain and humiliation. In this way the politics of humiliation is a very real threat to civilization, which depends not so much on "security" as on the continued utilization and enrichment of the accumulated wisdom of science, law, history, and diplomacy.

Humiliation of enemies is an ancient practice. It involves not only belittlement and ridicule but also demonization. Both are forms of dehumanization, for they imply that these persons are unfit for genuinely human society, and for genuine dialogue. Both forms of dehumanization were employed against Saddam, first portrayed as a paragon of evil and then pictured having lice removed from his disheveled hair. But this administration humiliates even allies and citizens—not only when they dare to criticize Pentagon policy, but even if they are only potential threats.

We can glimpse how the politics of humiliation works by considering an Iraqi who resents having a foreign soldier, who does not even speak his language, force his way at gunpoint into his home and search his private possessions. We would consider any American who offered no protest or resistance to such intrusion a coward, a real yellow-belly. But if the Iraqi resists, or even protests, he is branded a "terrorist" and becomes subject to melting into a mere statistic. (Simone Weil said that violence turns humans into things, but we now turn them into statistics instead—except in the cases where we don't even bother to count.)

The word "terrorist" is one of the tools of the politics of humiliation. All the prisoners at Abu Ghraib were "terrorists" or "potential terrorists." So they were not any longer "human."

This administration has vastly extended the ancient practice of humiliating enemies by vastly increasing the category of "enemy." It has done so in two ways. One is to include as an "enemy" any neutral person. In September of 2001 President Bush decreed that there could be no neutrals in the "war" against terror; so anyone who did not join with him was a friend of the terrorists, and hence an enemy. Germany and France were bad-mouthed as "old Europe," and the UN weapons inspectors were dismissed as a "failure." The other is to include as an "enemy" anyone who is a potential enemy, or a potential "terrorist." By that device the whole population of the world is subject to petty humiliations at every airport, at every US consulate, and at every port of entry. It is a humiliation to have one's things pawed over by strangers, even when they smile and act "professionally," as the TSA inspectors now do. Dignity and autonomy, the backbone of old-fashioned American freedom, vanish, suppressed by Ashcroft paternalism.

Life is certainly impoverished by Ashcroft paternalism, as by Rumsfeldian arrogance, but I see no reason to believe that the petty humiliations make us more secure.

The Cure

The cure for a politics of humiliation is twofold: it requires both humility and respect—listening to critics and protesters instead of cursing dissident Iraqis and skeptical senators. For those of us who see every person as among "all God's creatures," the demonization that underlies this politics of humiliation is a blasphemy, and part of the cure lies in an earnest search for that of God in each person, friend or foe. Jefferson's secular version is that every person has a moral sense that is as much a human organ as an arm or a leg, and as much in need of exercise; so respect for others means calling on their moral sense and giving them space to exercise it.

We don't know what is best for Iraq, On the other hand, it is obvious that what we are doing in Iraq is bad for the USA. The imperialist arrogance makes us foolish, the priority of military force over diplomacy makes us brutish, and using young Americans as instruments of the politics of humiliation corrupts our youth. It is time to end the whole ill-conceived adventure.

(10 May 2003)

6   Idolatry

The most common image of idolatry is the golden calf that Aaron made while Moses was absent on the mountain, and it is reported (Ex. 32:27-29) that its worship led to the slaughter of some 3,000 idolatrous Israelites by the Levites. The lesson is made explicit (Ex. 34:14-15): "You shall not prostrate yourself to any other god. For the Lord's name is the Jealous God, and a jealous god he is." Anyone searching the Scriptures can find many other instances of idols and idolatry, but the golden calf remains the popular paradigm.

We live in a sea of idolatry, worshiping, paying tribute to, trusting and depending on, and submitting to false gods. As a quick list of the false gods I am tempted to offer a catalog of seven P's: Princes, Politicians, Priests, Preachers, Police, Prisons, Pentagon.

It is a tentative list because I am not a seasoned prophet, and I lack the rhetorical certainty a true prophet needs. It is never easy to know how to apply a paradigm, since all applications occur far removed from the original circumstances. The image of the golden calf leaves us, for all its appeal, unclear about what constitutes worship and what makes something an unworthy object of worship even though it does have real value. I think it is helpful for understanding both our society and the resurgent fundamentalism to say that we generally bow down to and pay tribute to the seven P's, but saying that deserves closer scrutiny.

Worship

Worship is one of those grand things we often speak of with little understanding of what we are really saying. What is worship, really? We might start with forms of worship, the most distinctive of which are kneeling and prostration. Kneeling or prostration puts one in a defenseless and submissive posture, in recognition of a greater power to which one submits. For worship to be religious, in a way that binds the community together, there must also be rites or rituals of obeisance in which people participate together, where absence and other forms of nonparticipation count as disloyalty or apostasy, perhaps punishable by death. Furthermore, worship normally involves tribute (e.g., tithing), which serves to enhance either symbolically or really the power of the object of worship. Throughout the Scriptures we find the practice of these forms toward false gods condemned as idolatry.

Why is it not idolatry when a man on the Honors List kneels before the Queen? Only because the Queen, with popular consent, has relegated unto herself to serve as head of the Church of England, protector of the faith, and God's chief representative within the realm. To a Puritan the ritual of knighthood is indeed idolatry.

Idolatry cannot come into play without a recognition that the proper object of worship is God. In Islam this core idea is present in the Islamic ideal of prostrating oneself only to God, and never submitting oneself in like manner to any human authority. The practice of Islam may fail of this ideal where caliphs or sultans or mullahs seek recognition that borders on idolatry—the very sort of idolatry they see Catholics bestowing on the Pope. But the ideal of worshiping only God, trusting only in God, submitting only to God, is a powerful ideal that breeds courage and even heroism in true believers, not only in Islam but throughout the Abrahamic religions. There are thousands of stories of persons who remain heroically steadfast, submitting only to what is divine. My own favorite is that of Franz Jägerstätter, an Austrian peasant who refused to participate in Hitler's godless war and was consequently beheaded in Berlin in August, 1943 (See Gordon Zahn, *In Solitary Witness*). A similar heroism on the part of Thomas Becket is celebrated in T. S. Eliot's *Murder in the Cathedral*.

The root of this conception of worship is found throughout the Old Testament. It is expressed succinctly in the opening verse of Psalms 46: "God is our refuge and strength, a very present help in trouble."

The second clause of this verse reminds us that times of troubles are just the times to turn to God, rather than times when we might be excused for turning instead to princely powers. To believe that God is my refuge and strength has never meant that I will thereby or therefore be preserved from such ravages as princely powers may inflict on me. It means that I will nevertheless not bow down to or pay tribute to those powers, whatever ravages they threaten. That is where heroes enter and martyrs are made.

False Gods

The very idea of idolatry involves that nothing earthly or human is worthy of worship. The idea itself entails an ideal, and indeed the very sort of ideal that religions have nourished. Jägerstätter, for example, was a devout practicing Catholic, and his resistance to Hitler came through his being able to see clearly (as his Bishop did not) that Naziism was incompatible with his faith. Everything human falls short of that ideal. So bowing down to something earthly or human, or having any such thing as one's ultimate master, or giving any such thing the first fruits of one's labor or one's uncompromising submission—that is idolatry.

No one can even conceive of idolatry without a commitment to something that transcends earthly arrangements. Uncompromising commitment to justice is insufficient, and may indeed itself be a form of idolatry. A charge of idolatry can only be brought by a prophet, someone calling the people back to their original and underlying faith.

The Old Testament, being full of prophets, is also full of charges of idolatry. Consider again Psalms 46, "God is our refuge and strength, a very present help in trouble." It clearly speaks to people suffering trial and tribulations. A closer look at the first clause provides some light on how false gods can be recognized:

> God is our refuge and strength.
> Our refuge and strength is our god.

Since the text is an identity or equation, we can turn it around and see the same idea from another perspective. Where do we turn in times of trials and tribulations? Where did we as a nation turn after 9/11? Where do we turn when we sense that our property is in danger? Or that youth will get out of hand? Or when people have defied the law? Or when we decide where a tenth portion of our wealth is to go? - Is it not to the seven P's? Do we not live in a society where a visiting Martian would say that "our refuge and strength" is entrusted to Princes, Politicians, Priests, Preachers, Police, Prisons and the Pentagon?

The Seven P's

Princes and Politicians regularly proclaim that we are in grave danger, and it is they who will protect and save us, if only we give them the funds and the faithful trust they need. Some may suggest that this is only the case where there are democratic elections, but one will find other forms of it in the Middle Ages and the Renaissance, as well as in non-Christian civilizations. Politicians' grab for power is regularly disguised as salvation for the rest of us, and popular consent may be obtained either tacitly or electorally. The election of 2004 absorbed billions of dollars, including a portion of my own wealth, and in earlier times the sums collected by the monarch were referred to as tribute.. There was little or no thought that the campaign contributions or imperial tribute should be given instead to God. On the contrary, Constantine had the brilliant idea of claiming that he, the consummate prince and emperor, was sanctified by the church and therefore was to be adored in the same manner and to same degree as the Bishop of Rome. Ever since, political heads have claimed divine blessing and have themselves thereby become new paradigms of idolatry.

George W's remarkably successful courting of religious sanction for his aggressive military actions shows that he is as much a student (perhaps by osmosis) of Church history as of Machiavelli. On September 14, 2001, which he had declared a national day of mourning, he made a rare visit to the National Cathedral in Washington and declared war. The Bishop of Washington might have—and to my mind should have—chastised the President for transforming mourning into vengeance and abusing the sanctity of the holy place. But perhaps his silence was arranged in advance. Even though less eloquent than the rabble-rousing sermon of Urban II at Clermont in 1095, which led to the first Crusade, or the more powerful and polished sermons of Bernard of Clairvaux at Vézelay and Speir in 1146, which fueled the Second Crusade, the silence was all that was needed to confer a religious blessing on the "war against terror" that led US troops into Afghanistan and Iraq. The Crusades were a despicable perversion of religious ideals, but President Bush astutely imitated their success in diverting public support and devotion to the princely military powers of the Presidency, newly sanctified, again, as "our refuge and strength."

Priests and preachers collect huge sums each week, largely on their claim to represent God. I have no doubt that many priests and preachers are admirably modest in their claims and really do help their flock to hear the voice of God. But there are many others who take center stage themselves. In this age of McLuhan the critic has upstaged the author, the interpretation claims priority over the text, the medium is the message, and adoration of the preacher or the pope takes priority over adoration of the Lord. And perhaps McLuhan is right, that this has always been the case, with the church as intermediary building uncountable riches and worldly power, pretending all the while that contributing to its worldly wealth is really a way—perhaps the best way—of paying tribute to God. The church and its potentates are worshiped; that can hardly be denied. Whether or not this worship is idolatry is too complex an issue to be undertaken here. But that there are priests and preachers who lead their flocks astray, into worshiping false gods of one sort or another, is not likely to be denied by even the most fervent of believers.

As to the police, I welcome them and all the other public servants as contributors to civilization, but I decline to honor them as "the thin blue line" that separates civilization from barbarity. Humans do at times commit barbarous atrocities, but sometimes the perpetrators are the police themselves. Unhealthy submission to police authority is common in the form of the refusal of police departments to allow civilian review boards, thus holding themselves above the law. A minor illustration of granting police immunity from the law occurred in Amherst, NY, in connection with a "bait and shoot" program to reduce the suburban deer population. The program was implemented, and everyone assumed that because Amherst is a densely populated suburb within a cluster of counties where no gun more powerful than a shotgun (with slugs for deer) may be used, residents would be safe. But a slug from a high-powered rifle penetrated the outer wall and lodged inside one residential home. People were outraged, of course, but it was explained that police were not subject to the restrictions that apply to hunters, and the policeman in question was therefore entirely within his rights to have used a high-powered rifle in the program. Exempting persons from the law is a way of treating them as objects of adoration, golden calves of a sort. So it is with the police.

Prisons have two distinctive features—they are brutally violent and they are politically sacrosanct. Paradoxical, perhaps, but it is a paradox inherent in false gods. All punishment is violent, since it is the deliberate infliction of pain or suffering on persons. If we fail to see the violence—as is generally the case—it is because we regard the punishment as justified. It is no doubt partly justified by some prior infraction on the part of the prisoner, but such infraction does not justify any and every sort of pain and suffering. To my mind what makes the violence justifiable is, at a minimum, that it is designed to make the criminal fit to re-enter society. In practice that is rarely the case, for while they are in prison inmates are generally treated by those in authority as unworthy to be in society, thereby reducing the chances of a successful re-entry. Politicians bow down to prisons, which play a role in state government analogous to that of the military in our national government. They constitute an ever-expanding and unexamined expenditure against which neither party dares raise a finger. The USA now has a higher proportion of its citizens in prison than any other civilized country, having in the past two decades surpassed South Africa and Russia, both of which reduced their prison populations after democratic revolutions. Sanity would suggest that we re-examine what prisons are for and whether we need to spend so much of our resources on them. But the only reform recently undertaken has been to "privatize" prisons without in any way calling into question their role as a "refuge and strength" against the trials and tribulations of civil society. On the contrary, they get worse. When George Pataki became governor of New York State, one of his first acts was to revise the rule that allowed inmates to enroll in college courses through the state's Tuition Assistance Program. This action substantially reduced the prognosis for successful re-entry into society after release from prison, but it placated resentful prison guards. Prisons are sacrosanct in America, and their personnel are like temple servants.

Of all the forms of idiolatry we practice in this country, our idolizing of the Pentagon is the most egregious. As with police and prisons, one can acknowledge that armed forces may sometimes be beneficial. I myself remain unconvinced, because the military establishments of the world generally consume rather than produce national wealth, and the benefits seem incidental and accidental (such as racial integration, and quality education for service families) rather than intrinsic to the mission. But let us grant that, in proportion, some level of defense force is indispensable for a modern nation. In the USA the expenditures are all out of proportion, and the continued increases are by any rational assessment insane. But of course it is not a matter of reason. Reason has been blinded by paranoia and drugged by our worship of the Pentagon as our only and true refuge and strength against "terrorism." We lay at the steps of the Pentagon the first fruits of our labor. Over half the national budget (excluding Social Security) goes for military expenditures, and in 2004 our military expenditures accounted for nearly half the world's total and exceeded the combined expenditures of the next fifteen countries. The Pentagon budget increases each year, sometimes more than the Pentagon requests, without regard to which party is in power and independently of how good or bad a job the Pentagon has done. Inefficiencies are mind-boggling but irrelevant. Disputes in Congress about Pentagon spending resemble instead disputes as to whether a goat or a lamb is the right offering to the god.

A visitor from Mars who understood the categories would have to conclude that the Pentagon is an object or worship rather than of practical reason. Our refusal to apply rational criticism and assessment to the budget and the practices of the Pentagon constitutes the foremost example of idolatry of our time.

The Voice of a Reluctant Prophet

Who am I to be talking about idolatry? A modern prophet? Another Ezekiel or Jeremiah? As mentioned earlier, it does take someone like a prophet to make charges of idolatry, since such charges entail commitment to God. It is a good question.

There are two answers to this sound query. One is that it takes only a thoughtful observer to notice the difference between worship and practical reason. Those categories are common enough, even though not well defined, and the difference between them is not so subtle that a thoughtful observer will be tricked by Pascal's Wager into confusing them.

The other part of the answer is that I am both a Quaker and a Jeffersonian. As a liberal Quaker I have little truck with theology or altars but I do believe that we live our lives in a divine presence, and that there is in every person something of God that George Fox referred to as the Light to live by or the Seed Christ. I have no objection to identifying this Light with the moral sense that Jefferson called as much an organ of a human being as an arm or a leg, and in as much need of exercise. It has been a part of my experience in this world that my refuge and strength lies in this moral sense or Seed Christ in others, and part of my conviction that all these forms of idolatry accorded to the seven P's denigrate this divinity, scoff at this sort of strength and security, and seek to replace it with their worldly powers.

The prophets were never voices of the mainstream, which at least since Constantine has regularly sanctified what I have labeled as idols. But the prophetic voices were embedded in tradition, not voices in the wilderness. Nor is my voice a voice in the wilderness. It is the voice, or one of the voices, of dedicated people all over the globe, in all sorts of cultures, who know (without relying on evidence) that there is something friendly and cooperative and immeasurably valuable in every person, and who seek to nurture and encourage that something through service, servant-leadership, education, and fellowship. Such people exemplify alternatives to the seven P's their service, leadership, and fellowship with strangers as well as with close companions are patterns and examples that eloquently undermine the false theology of the seven P's and attest to the old faith to which I mean to call people back. My naming of idols and false gods has roots in this broad and buoyant fellowship.

(10 May 2003)

II: Focus on Bolivia

7   Bolivia in Turmoil

I arrived in La Paz on Saturday October 11, 2003, just in time to witness the showdown between the campesinos and the government. These days have been, as Dickens famously wrote of the French Revolution, the best of times and the worst of times. I am writing this on Wednesday the 15th, the third day of a total shutdown in La Paz. Schools, banks, shops, and restaurants remain closed, and transport is shut down, but the kids are playing soccer and volleyball in the streets. In the tension of uncertainty, there is now peace and calm after the confrontations of Sunday and Monday, confrontations that left 54 people dead, raising the total since the confrontation started in August to about 70. This is the second major set of confrontations of the year, the other having occurred in February when 32 people died. So the total for the year is over 100, almost all campesinos.

Since Bolivia is little more than a name for most of us, it will be useful to provide some background and then discuss the issues that divide the country at the present time.

Background

Like most of Latin America Bolivia can be divided, with a little simplification, into city (*ciudad*) and country (*campo*), and the campesinos are the part of the population who identify with the country rather than the city. They may have moved to the city but still have roots in the country. There are also, of course, younger people, children of campesinos, who were born in the city and even have advanced degrees and who do not fall easily into either group; they are no longer real campesinos but identify more with them than with the government.

The division between city and country is accompanied by an ethnic difference, the difference between the indigenous peoples and the people with substantial European (mostly Spanish) heritage. The campesinos are wholly indigenous, and it has always been the people of European descent who have ruled the cities and held the reins of political power. During the Spanish period the indigenous peoples were mostly slaves on estates —bought and sold as part of the estates—and it was not until the revolution of 1952 that they could legally be educated.

For decades Bolivia has been the poorest country in South America, with the possible exception of Guyana. The poverty is of course not equally distributed, falling most oppressively on the campesinos. The economic disparities are enormous. The downturn in the world economy, and especially the economic troubles in Brazil and Argentina, have wreaked havoc with the Bolivian economy, and especially with the campesinos.

The current president, Gonzalo Sánchez de Lozada, is of course of European descent, as are all the members of his cabinet who appeared on television last night. He is not prejudiced, and during his previous term (1993-97) both the Minister and the Under-minister of Education had indigenous rather than European roots. But Sánchez de Lozada is further distanced from the population here by having spent his formative years in the USA, graduating from a Quaker boarding school in Iowa and then studying at the University of Chicago. He speaks Spanish with an American accent.

CAMPESINOS.

The campesinos are people with roots in the country rather than the city, wherever they may live. El Alto is city of some 800,000, all of whom should be considered campesinos. The campesinos are all lower-class indigenous people, and their mother tongue is generally one of the 23 indigenous languages rather than Spanish. Some indigenous people are no longer campesinos; those who were born in the city, have Spanish as their mother tongue, and have become doctors or lawyers or other middle-class professionals.

Even though Bolivia has the largest proportion of indigenous people in the hemisphere—about 70%, followed by Guatemala—the campesinos have never had any significant political power. They mostly eke out a living on small farms, bringing goods to market in the city. They are the oppressed of the oppressed, with an average annual income under $600, and with houses lacking running water and electricity. A huge proportion are malnourished, and education and health services are primitive. But they are lively and industrious and not generally sullen.

There have been campesino protests or uprisings each year for the past eight or ten years, over different issues. The campesino tactic has been to block highways, generally highways on the Altiplano that are used to supply La Paz. The blockades are primitive, made of local rocks, but they have become increasingly effective politically.

Over the past half-dozen years the two most effective campesino leaders (both now members of Congress) have been Evo Morales, president of the cocaleros (farmers in Chapare who grew coca leaves for export to Colombia), and Felipe Quispe (also known as "el Mallku," which means boss condor in Aymara), whose power base is among the Aymara campesinos in the Altiplano (around Lake Titicaca). They are the spokesmen to whom the media turn. But in fact they are able to speak for only a small fraction of the campesinos. One Bolivian friend put it this way: "Evo and Mallku were calling the shots last week, but they lost control on Sunday night; the mass movement we are witnessing today has many, many leaders, but no coordinated leadership overall."

THE ISSUES

There are two issues in the current showdown. One is how to use the enormous reserves of natural gas that have been discovered in Bolivia. This is the issue around which the showdown began in August. The other issue is the president himself, and it is this issue that has moved into the foreground in recent days.

GAS

The first gas was discovered in 1924. There were further discoveries over the years in the southern part of the country and the full extent of the reserves has gradually become known. A dozen years ago plans were begun by the multinational Repsol-YPF to pipe the gas to the coast, liquify it, and sell it to California. Much pipeline has now been built, but it does not reach the coast. In the intervening years, especially in the past half dozen years, it has been determined that the reserves are some fifty times larger than originally estimated, and there has been increasing discussion about selling off the national riches.

There are two main issues about the envisaged sale. One is that the exploitation of the mineral wealth of the country would mostly enrich Chileans and international corporations rather than Bolivians. The other is that the proposed route of the pipeline would benefit Chile, an historic enemy since Chile took away Bolivia's outlet to the sea in the Charko War 125 years ago.

Quispe galvanized the campesinos around this issue in August, arguing it was time to put an end to the wealth of Bolivia being used to enrich the rest of the world, time for it to be used to enrich Bolivians. So the campesinos demanded that the sale of gas to, or through, Chile be canceled, and that the gas be used instead for industrialization within Bolivia. To enforce the demands they blockaded the roads north of La Paz, through the Aymara strongholds of Warisata and Achicachi to the tourist center of Sorata.

The first serious confrontation took place later in the month when the army forcibly evacuated some hundred foreign tourists from Sorata, leaving six dead in Warisata.

Facts about the gas.

The facts are not easy to come by, and I rely largely on a manifesto from the "consejo universitario" of the Universidad Mayor de San Andrés, the main public university of Bolivia, which is dated yesterday and was published in today's edition of La Razon. The proven reserves are now 60 trillion cubic feet (TCF) and likely to reach 150 TCF, a quantity sufficient to supply an industrialized Bolivia for 600 years. When the reserves were contracted to Repsol-YPF some years ago, the sale was on a lump sum basis rather than on the amount of gas extracted, and the lump sum was based on only 2 TCF, the proven reserve at the time but a very small fraction of the true reserve as it is now known. Furthermore Bolivia was to receive only 18% of the proceeds.

The terms of the sale were not based on legislation but on a presidential decree, DS 24806, issued by President Gonzalo Sánchez de

Lozada just two days before he left office at the end of his first term in 1997. The manifesto calls this decree unconstitutional and says that its revocation is essential to a solution of the problem about gas.

The dispute about gas becomes clearer when we see that there four distinct issues that affect the national pride and national well-being:

— that the gas is being exported rather than used locally,
— that the exportation takes place through Chile,
— that the contract price was based on only 2 TCF of gas,
— that Bolivia receives 18% rather than 50% of proceeds.

These are powerful issues that are being articulated with increasing clarity and cogency.

The President

"Goni," as he is called, is not a cruel or evil man, but he is not politically astute and seems to have got himself into an impossible position. He is a wealthy man, he believes in free enterprise and free markets, and he takes the US as a model for what he would like Bolivia to become. His most powerful support seems to come from abroad; and though he won about 23% of the vote in the election last year, he lacks a natural political base in the country.

His first problem is that he is seen as the father of the nefarious gas deal. It is a rather typical sort of free enterprise deal; it will, if implemented, bring money to Bolivia, and he probably has trouble seeing that there is anything wrong with it. I doubt that George Bush or Dick Cheney would see anything wrong with it either. Perhaps his belief in free enterprise amounts to what Paul Krugman has called "free enterprise fundamentalism." At any rate, it is what left the opening for Quispe to begin the confrontation in August.

The president then used force to break through the blockade. Most US officials would have done the same, and the casualties were considerably fewer than when Janet Reno decided to use force to end the stalemate at Waco. But Reno's victims were an insignificant sect with no political power, whereas Goni's victims were Aymara campesinos whose death inflamed Quispe's power base. Furthermore the evacuation of the tourists worsened the main problem: it made dialogue more difficult, so that the road remains closed to traffic to this day.

Again last Sunday the president decided to use force to replenish gasoline supplies in the capital, and this time there were 34 deaths. Mallku and others were already calling for his renunciation of power, and now the calls increased. His vice-president publicly withdrew his support, and the mayor of La Paz has called for him to step down. Whereas at first it seemed as though it was the campesinos against the establishment, now the establishment is divided with a substantial part calling for his resignation.

On Tuesday the president made a firm statement, praised by La Razón, calling for dialogue, urging national unity and support of democratic institutions, insisting that all the terms for the sale of gas were open for discussion, and refusing to resign. But the opposition had hardened, dialogue was just what he had spurned when he broke through the blockades in Warisata and El Alto, and the massive popular movement calling for resignation considers itself the voice of democracy. The president was scheduled to make a statement at 9 this morning, but he canceled it, and this afternoon there are again massive demonstrations in the center of the city, this time with huge explosions, since the Bolivian miners use dynamite for firecrackers.

THE EVENTS

Sunday was tense, with rumors that something was going to happen. I went to the Quaker church in the morning, but the Friends insisted that I go right back. In the evening there was the confrontation in El Alto, with 34 deaths. There were immediate calls for the president's resignation and for marches on the capital the next day. Monday the marches began in mid-morning, converging on the center from several directions, and there were another 20 people killed. By Monday evening things were more calm, but there were bonfires at many intersections. There seemed to be a stand-off: the armed forces remained loyal to the president and had turned back the militants, but the city remained paralyzed.

On Sunday night the opposition had called for an indefinite shutdown of the whole country as well as of La Paz, and the transport workers called for a 72-hour shutdown of transport. Even though Goni won the show of force on Monday, he has not been able to end the shutdown. According to the paper, Sucre, Cochabamba, Oruru, and Potosi are all paralyzed, as well as La Paz and El Alto. That leaves Santa Cruz and Tarija as the only major cities leading a more or less normal life.

This morning there was activity in the market three blocks away, cut flowers and camomile being especially plentiful. Tonight I heard that the airport will be closed tomorrow for the fourth day.

The Outcome

There is such uncertainty about what will happen next that many embassies have urged that all tourists leave La Paz. I wonder how that could possibly be done. It now seems that the only thing that would restore calm, at least for a moment, is the president's resignation, but most international organizations continue supporting him as the legitimate democratic leader. The past two days have been relatively calm, but there is an underlying tension caused by the uncertainty.

The opposition, especially the campesinos, refer to the president as an "assassin" and speak of the killings; they call for an end to killing and also for the "assassin" to acknowledge his wrongs and step down. The president and his cabinet regard the blockades as a form of violence, and call for an end to violence. There is truth to both sides. Neither such killings nor such blockades can be part of civilized society. Nor can this eerie shutdown. So far there seems blame enough to be shared around, and not much in creative innovation.

Tonight the president made a joint declaration with two of his opposition candidates in the 2002 election, Jaime Paz Zamora (a former president) and Fernando Villa Reyes (head of a right-wing party). More than anything else it represents a last-ditch coalition to hold on to the old order. It may succeed for now, with its international backing and its claim to legitimacy. But it was immediately rejected by campesino leaders, and the massiveness of the marches and protests shows that change is exactly what cannot be avoided for long.

The issue about gas has now been demoted to second rank, though it is of first importance in the long run. There are bound to be legal complications about it, including the status of DS 24806 and of the contract with Repsol-YPF, and the WTO could end up penalizing Bolivia for any revocation or substantial revision. But these events have dramatically heightened a sense of national treasure and national heritage, as well as of opportunity, and the issue is not likely to disappear. The best chance for the current plans to proceed would be for Gonzalo Sanchez to overcome his opposition, and that may partly explain his international support.

It is difficult to see how the city can return to normal without the president resigning. His resignation would end the shutdown and begin the return to normal. The president has called for dialogue, which is not likely to occur, but has given no indication of what steps he could or might take to end the shutdown. He has the police and the military, but they failed to end the shutdown on Monday, and it difficult to see how they could do so now. The president lacks the political power necessary to use his military power, and the new coalition announced tonight seems insufficient to the tasks.

However the current issues are resolved, one inescapable result of the events of 2003 is the enormously increased political power of the indigenous people. For that alone this year will go down as a banner year in Bolivian history. No indigenous politician will assume the highest office just now, but the establishment has much to fear. Redistribution of wealth is only one of the threats. Evo believes in free market policies for coca and cocaine, and would rescind the eradication of coca for export that has been achieved over the past ten years. And Mallku has fomented an Aymara nationalism that not only calls for an independent Aymara nation but also insists that all "gringos" leave Bolivia. (Vague threats connected with this last point were a factor prompting the evacuation of the tourists from Sorata.) Fortunately events seem to have overtaken these now somewhat stale campesino leaders, but we have little idea what will come next.

It is well to recognize that change is not always for the best. But it is for the best to recognize change when it is at hand and to adjust policies to accommodate it.

— La Paz, 10.15.03

Addendum - 10.16.03.

Two points.
(1) Reports abroad that the necessities of life are unavailable in La Paz need qualification. The neighborhood where I am staying is one where no foreigners or middle-class Bolivians live. Here there are no supermarkets, but the large market down the street has everything one might need, other than bread, albeit at vastly elevated prices: meat has doubled and eggs tripled in price. (The higher prices go directly into the pockets of campesinos.) There are no long lines, as there are at supermarkets. Supermarkets, on the other hand, have limited supplies (no transport to resupply them), limited hours, and long lines. So the middle class and expatriates may be suffering more than the lower class.

(2) Thousands more campesinos marched into the capital today in an amazing demonstration of their determination that the president resign. Among others there were 4,000 who arrived in the morning from the Yungas and 8,000 who arrived mid-day from El Alto. I watched the second march, which took some 20 minutes to pass. It was entirely peaceful, with no shots or explosions or vandalism, and it was composed of campesinos of both sexes and all ages; later I encountered a small part of them resting in front of my hotel, and sensed no reason at all for fear. Seeing these people heightened my sense that Goni cannot outlast the shutdowns that he cannot end.

(17 October 2003)

8   Bolivia at a Crossroads

In a previous essay, "Bolivia in Turmoil" (Buffalo Report October 17, 2003), written during the week of demonstrations and marches that led to the resignation of President Gonzalo Sánchez de Lozada on Friday October 17, I argued that the one sure result would be vastly increased power of the campesinos. But power to block things and power to achieve things are two entirely different sorts of power. It now remains to be seen whether Bolivia has friends who will help assure that the newly confirmed powers will be used constructively, in ways that will not exacerbate divisions and animosities.

The Disaster Model of Equatorial Guinea

On November 16, "60 Minutes" aired a program about Equatorial Guinea, another country with recently discovered fossil fuel reserves. There is no question that money has flowed into the country, which now has embassies that give lavish parties. But the money has produced increased oppression rather than affluence and well-being, since the funds are controlled by the president, largely for the benefit of himself and his family. There are, of course, occasional handouts. But there is no free press and no opportunity for public scrutiny of the scandalous waste of public assets. The principal energy company, Exxon Mobil, knows that it is financing tyranny, but apparently (it declined an invitation from "60 Minutes") regards its collusion with the dictator as a fair price to pay for the stability needed to exploit the offshore oil deposits. Might that happen in Bolivia?

Certainly Bolivia is a different country with different traditions, and its future remains open. On the one hand there are forces working on the pattern Exxon Mobil has established in Equatorial Guinea. The popular opposition to President Sánchez saw his policy as moving in that direction. They regarded Bolivia's 18% share of the proceeds as too small -- in Equatorial Guinea it is only 12% -- and they saw the bulk of the poor people in Bolivia being neglected for the sake of big profits of foreigners who are already rich. On the other hand there is already a free press in Bolivia, and a vigorous political tradition with campesino power. I think it unlikely that the deal in Bolivia would have been as bad as that in Africa. But the pattern did indeed look similar.

Distortions in The Times

There is perhaps an equal danger in Bolivia that the winner to emerge out the turmoil of October will be an indigenous leader who will establish an indigenous dictatorship. That is the danger of which Sánchez warned in his resignation letter, a warning which was echoed in a New York Times editorial of November 3, "Revolt of the Poor in Bolivia." "Not since the arrival of the Spanish conquistadores have Latin America's Indians enjoyed the political influence they have today." says the Times. "Sadly, however, the indigenous may not benefit. Leaders of the Bolivia protests, for example, advocate policies that would make the poor worse off." After noting that part of the popular movement that carried the day was a backlash against globalization, the Times concludes, "The nationalism and economic ignorance of the opposition to the gas deal show where the indigenous movement is going wrong. . . they must distance themselves from a counterproductive populism and develop economic policies that really work to help the poor."

Opposing ignorance falls into the same class as favoring motherhood and apple pie. But what is the "ignorance" the Times complains of? Just what are the economic policies of the indigenous movement? The Times notes the long history of wrongs, culminating in anger over Washington's insistence on eradicating the profitable cash crop of coca. But the only hint of an economic policy they cite is: "Many Bolivians do not want their country to sell its gas at all."

I do not know whether it is true that "many Bolivians do not want their country to sell its gas at all." Rhetoric to that effect did occur during September and October, even on the part of members of Congress. There is a vagueness about "many" that makes the statement impossible to refute. Nonetheless the picture that it conveys is wholly misleading. It is as if one were to say that many Americans believe that there should be no restrictions at all on the possession and use of firearms. Not provably false, but highly misleading.

Bias in the Washington Diplomat

A report on Bolivia in the Washington Diplomat for December 2003 contains similar understandable errors – understandable because of the general ignorance of the press about Bolivia and the tendency to try to find the key players. That is not to excuse the errors, since they do betray a bias or two, and may also impede progress.

Where the Violence Was

One of the problems is the emphasis at the beginning of the story on the days of violent demonstrations. The problems started with blockades, which have been ruled a form of violence in German law (the cases involved sit-ins at entrances to munitions plants), and which are at least a form of confrontation. The deaths were initially caused not by demonstrations but by the government deciding to break the blockades by armed force. The first such attempt was in August or September, when tourists were evacuated from Sorata, a center for trekking. No deaths were directly due to demonstrators; the army killed a dozen or so. The second attempt came on the fateful day of October 12, when the army attempted to escort a convoy of trucks to replenish fuel supplies in La Paz, a confrontation that resulted in 34 deaths. Those deaths led at first to angry demonstrations the next day, leading to property damage in the streets (mostly paving stones removed for barricades against military reprisal; little or no looting) and 20 more deaths. The overall death toll is generally put at 70, among whom there was only one soldier/policeman.

The following days there were more demonstrations, culminating with 100,000 people in Plaza San Francisco on Thursday, the day before the resignation of President Sánchez, and the decisive day politically. There was again some property damage to hotels near Plaza Murillo, but the marches themselves showed discipline and determination and were entirely peaceful. In these days the main cry was for the resignation of the president, driven home at times by calling him a killer, and a prominent secondary slogan was that there should be no more blood shed. The generally pacific nature of the marches and demonstrations does not come through in the reporting in the Diplomat or the Times.

Complexity of Indigenous Leadership

Another distortion is that only one peasant leader is named as a leader, Evo Morales. He is important. He is leader of the coca growers (*cocaleros*), enjoys the support of the miners and several other unions, is a member of Congress, and came in second to Sánchez de Lozada in the presidential polling in 2002. But the original protest was against the terms of the gas sale, and that was not initiated by Morales but by Felipe Quispe (known as "El Mallku", "condor" in Aymara), also a member of Congress and the spokesman for the campesinos in the altiplano north of La Paz. (Morales has his base in the Chapare, south of La Paz and at a much lower elevation.) It is also Quispe who has developed the tactic of blockades, using them each year with increasing effectiveness. When Quispe's campaign began to hit home last summer, Morales joined in and has not been reluctant to take credit; he has a much better public relations staff.

The Understanding of Exploitation

Though the campesinos are often thought to be ignorant, and indeed have poor schools, it will be wise to note the sophistication of Quispe's understanding of the gas deal as another instance of the exploitation of Bolivia's natural resources. Beginning with the Spanish, if not with the Incas, such exploitation has in the past resulted in increased wealth for foreign exploiters and increased oppression for the indigenous people. The powerful popular response to Quispe's campaign demonstrates that this historical understanding is deep and constitutes a significant political factor today.

A Variety of Problems

The problem with this second distortion is that it leads commentators to say that the main issue in Bolivia is the US insistence on eradicating coca production, without effective alternative work for the cocaleros. That is a problem, but solving it will do nothing to satisfy Quispe and the campesinos whose complaints he voices. There are two problems that are thereby obscured: the plight of the campesinos in the altiplano north of La Paz, and the terms of the gas sale. Each of these is as important as the problems Morales and his constituents press.

The new president, Carlos Mesa, is a fresh face in national politics, and one must wish him well, as is done in the Diplomat. But wishing him well may not be enough. He faces the same problems as Sánchez, who, of course, could hardly take the underlying problems away with him when he left for Florida. In fact Sánchez has probably made them more difficult, by portraying those who forced him out as ignorant and irrational. His perspective is reflected not only in his letter of resignation but also in the New York Times editorial of November 3, which claims, as noted above, that "nationalism and economic ignorance of the opposition to the gas deal show where the indigenous movement is going wrong." This perspective is a prescription for disaster.

Toward a Positive Future

There are two truths that must be in President Mesa's mind and that need to anchor thoughts and policies toward Bolivia now:
 —Failing to export some of the huge reserves of natural gas spells economic suicide.
 —Failing to revise the terms of the sale spells political suicide.
Given these two policy anchors, what is needed is help and advice about how to redefine the deal. Since the international consortium is reported to have already spent $3 billion developing the wells and the pipeline, delicate and complex negotiation will be required.

I read the daily La Razón every day during the week of work stoppage, marches, and demonstrations that led to the resignation of Sánchez de Lozada. (Even though churches, schools, banks, post offices, laundries, restaurants, shops were all closed, and street vendors absent and transport unavailable, all the media continued operations—a healthy sign indeed.) Economic ideas that appeared in the press included basing the gas deal on current (150 trillion cubic feet) rather than 1997 (2 TCF) proven reserves, raising Bolivia's share of the proceeds from 18% to 50%, using gas for industrialization before exporting it, assuring benefits for Bolivia's poor up front rather than down the line. There were other points raised about the gas deal that were more political than these, but these points were voiced with several variations.

My own sense of what is desirable for revising the gas deal is that it should include three features:

(1) something like 80% of the jobs at every level reserved for Bolivians, with training provided wherever necessary and even if this means some delay in the project;

(2) immediate development of plans for small-scale industrialization in at least three cities, Tarija, Cochabamba, and El Alto, with immediate jobs and job training; and

(3) immediate up-front infrastructure improvements (schools, roads, water, power) for the altiplano, using (and training) local labor wherever possible.

President Mesa and his country will need considerable international help in achieving a revision along these lines, but such a revision could well provide an international model for resource exploitation in other places.

(5 December 2003)

9 The Anti-political Politician: Reflections on Bolivia

Bolivia is blessed not only with gorgeous scenery that ranges from Amazonian rainforest to the High Andes but also by being generally ignored by the press of the northern hemisphere. Searching for "Bolivia" in the New York Times online, I often go months without having any new hits, save for an occasional item where Bolivia is included as one of a number of Latin American countries. The past 18 months has been different. In October 2003 the elected president, Sánchez de Lozada, was forced to resign: using the army to break a campesino blockade of the capital backfired. The Indians all around the country, not just around the capital, responded with mass demonstrations and peaceful marches, exhibiting discipline and determination for which the President had no response. (See Buffalo Report postings of 17 November 2003 "Bolivia in Turmoil" and 5 December 2003 "Bolivia at a Crossroads".) He fled the country and was replaced by his vice-president, Carlos Mesa. Carlos Mesa has proved to be an imaginative anti-political politician, surviving longer than any of the pundits conceived possible.

POLITICS AND ANTI-POLITICS

I had better explain my terms. Politics has to do with securing, exercising, and retaining power, where power is understood as domination and control of the institutions and resources of a nation-state or other political entity, by what means are available. It is in the spirit of such a conception of politics that Clausewitz said that war is an extension of politics by other means. In gaining control of a nation-state, a politician gains control of powerful instruments of coercion, including the treasury, the army, the police, the secret service, and the prisons. In totalitarian states the press, the churches, and the judiciary are included among the instruments of political power, and even in the United States we often see a yearning by the administration for control these institutions that our Constitution separates from the seat of political power. It is normal for presidents and other political leaders to employ whatever instruments of persuasion and coercion are available.

Philip Pettit, the Australian philosopher, has said that we cannot understand the working of modern society, particularly the workings of democracy, unless we supplement this basic conception of politics and power with an understanding of anti-power. Anti-power has to do with limits on the use and employment of the ordinary instruments of political power. It comes in two main forms, limitations on what politicians actually do, and limitations on what politicians are authorized to do. The U.S. Constitution not only establishes political powers but also establishes limits on political powers, particularly through the separation of powers, States' Rights, and the first ten amendments (the Bill of Rights). These provisions have led to the independence of the judiciary, the press, and religion, the courts becoming an instrument for ensuring and elaborating these limitations. Our democracy has also been blessed by the establishment of independent institutions, such as the ACLU, whose whole purpose is to promote anti-power, that is to be anti-political. Just as politics is the exercise of power, anti-politics is the exercise of anti-power.

None of our presidents, with the possible exceptions of Washington and Jefferson, has been anti-political. If we look at recent elections, we see that the attempt to secure power is highly partisan and involves intensive and detailed work by political parties at every level. Carl Schmitt has said (in *The Concept of the Political*) that politics begins with a distinction between friends and enemies. He had nation-states in mind, but we can see this phenomenon clearly in the partisan character of electoral politics. Washington became president without a partisan campaign, but nothing similar has happened in the past 200 years. The election of 1800 between Jefferson and Adams was highly partisan and divisive, and today we cannot imagine a democratic election that does not involve political parties and all the divisive partisan activity they entail.

THE UNELECTED PRESIDENT

Let us return to Bolivia. Carlos Mesa is president of a democratic country, but he was not elected to be President. Nor does he lead a political party that might constitute his political base. He has no political base. There are numerous political parties in Bolivia, half a dozen that have played a significant role in recent elections. None of these parties put forward Mesa as a candidate for the presidency, each having put forward instead its own candidate. Sánchez de Lozada chose him as a running-mate in 2002, probably as a way to attract support from outside his party and from outside politics. Mesa had been a historian and a television journalist, and he was known to the public through his writings and through television. He had led no party, he never held any political office, nor had he any experience as the executive of any large institution. No one expected him to become president, and few thought him capable of it. He therefore came into politics from outside of politics—non-political but not yet anti-political.

As the events of October 2003 unfolded, Mesa immediately deplored the use of the army to break the blockade, and the next day withdrew his support of Sánchez de Lozada. He did not, however, resign. When Sánchez resigned, Mesa therefore came to power by right of constitutional succession. He did not seek the endorsement of the outgoing president's party or of any other party, but remained as president with no ability through party affiliation to wield a block of votes in parliament. Many people doubted whether he would long remain in office, since in spite of his constitutional legitimacy he lacked both democratic (electoral) legitimacy and political support.

Carlos Mesa and the Indians

It was the Bolivian Indians who had done in Sánchez, and Mesa undertook three significant measures to try to stave off Indian opposition to his policies. The first was to promise a referendum on the exploitation of the huge resources of natural gas, and the referendum was duly held last year. The second was to undertake to improve the infrastructure in the indigenous city of EL Alto. He has not succeeded in finding a way to provide drinking water and sewage because of the high capital costs, but both the main roads and the side streets in EL Alto have been significantly improved in the past eighteen months. In November 2004, I visited a Quaker school on one of those side streets, and the formerly dirt roadway was being replaced—expertly and expeditiously—with an impressive cobblestone street. This project uses only local materials, and it not only improves the appearance and accessibility of the neighborhood, but also is a labor-intensive project that helps reduce unemployment. Mesa's third undertaking was anti-political: he vowed not to use the army or the police to break up roadblocks or peaceful demonstrations.

When Bolivia hit the front page of the New York Times again in February/March 2005, it was because of a confrontation between President Mesa and Evo Morales, the most prominent Indian politician in Bolivia, leader of a socialist party known as MAS, leader also of the unions of miners and of coca farmers, and the candidate who came in second to Sánchez de Lozada in the 2002 elections. The issue, besides being a contest of power, concerned the exploitation of the reserves of natural gas.

For at least two years, Morales has demanded that the royalties on the extraction of natural gas be raised to 50 %, and the roadblocks of 2003 were meant to enforce that demand. President Mesa found this demand unacceptable, but he did believe, especially following the referendum, that the revenues to Bolivia for the exploitation of the gas needed to be raised. He therefore held extensive discussions with officials of the international consortium and others, and proposed a law enacting a new energy policy. The new law proposes no change in the division of royalties, but proposes a dramatic increase in the tax on profits from the exploitation of gas, to 32%. It was at this point that Morales withdrew his support from President Mesa.

The Triumph of Anti-Politics

So far, everything is normal relatively politics.

Bolivia made the news when President Mesa responded with an anti-political gesture: he sent a letter to the legislature submitting his resignation. In some sort of broad fuzzy sense of politics, such a letter might be thought a political gesture or tactic. When one regards it seriously, however, one sees that it is not an exercise of power or a utilization of the instruments of power but a resignation from power and the instruments or power. In the event it did secure for President Mesa declarations of support from all the major political parties with the exception of MAS. Evo Morales and his supporters among the impoverished Indian population on the Altiplano restored the roadblocks that has been their most effective political instrument over the past five or six years, a powerful form of coercion . In the face of this confrontation, President Mesa steadfastly refused to become political. He reiterated his refusal to order the army to clear the roads, declared that he had done everything that he knew how to do and that the country was ungovernable with its main roads blocked, and so he would ask Congress to call early elections to find someone as his replacement.

At this point Morales began to see his power ebb away. During a two-day strike he had called to protest the new energy law, teachers continued to meet their classes although they constitute the third or fourth largest union; so his base shrank. In addition Morales did not want Mesa to leave the presidency, recognizing that any replacement would use armed force to break the blockades and open the roads. So the roadblocks were removed by the Indians who had put them in place. President Mesa withdrew the bill to establish early elections and he remains in office with a remarkably high approval rating in the polls, about 60%.

If Bolivia were not such an obscure country, Carlos Mesa would be a good candidate for the Nobel Peace Prize. Politics is inherently divisive, and although we cannot do without it, it can never lead to peace. Nor can we expect that there will be very many, if any, anti-political politicians in positions of authority. Simone Weil said that it is a natural necessity that politicians should employ political power, and therefore a miracle when a politician acts anti-politically. Perhaps it is. Certainly we cannot expect other politicians to follow the example of Carlos Mesa. But he does deserve recognition and admiration.

(26 March 2005)

10 Bolivia: Preparing the Third Revolution

During the past two weeks there has again been an intense combination of turmoil and opportunity in Bolivia. The news reports have sometimes compared these recent events with those of October 2003, but the differences are significant and this year's crisis cannot be resolved so easily as that of 2003. The main event in 2005 is a power play by the Indians of Bolivia, led by the Aymara, but there is also a counter power play by free-market entrepreneurs of Santa Cruz. The events of 2003 are indeed part of the prelude, but we cannot understand what is happening without taking note of the centuries of Spanish oppression, the earlier revolutions of 1952 and 1982, and differences between 2003 and 2005.

The Spaniards treated all of the Indians of South America as slaves, and people of European ancestry continue to compose the elite of Bolivia and to hold the reigns of power, even though indigenous peoples constitute between 65% and 70% of the population. The Indians were never content with their subjugation, but it is only since 1952 that there has been steady progress toward overcoming it.

During the 1940s several leftist-oriented political parties were organized. The most important of these was the Nationalist Revolutionary Movement (Movimiento Nacionalista Revolucionario, or MNR), founded by young nationalist intellectuals and headed by Victor Paz Estenssoro, an economist and one-time close adviser to a previous president. The MNR opposed the power of the big mining companies and advocated freeing the Indian people from exploitation. In 1943 the MNR led a successful coup, encouraged unionization of tin mines, and tried to improve Indian living conditions. These efforts brought conflict with the tin barons, culminating in a bloody uprising in La Paz in 1946, and for the next six years the government remained in the hands of conservatives.

The First Revolution

In 1951, even though exiled in Argentina, Victor Paz won nearly half the presidential election vote. To prevent his installation, the government was placed under the control of a military junta. In 1952 a revolution by the MNR and the miners put him in the presidency, and the MNR began its program of profound social, economic, and political changes. It pledged to make the Indians full-fledged members of the national community, to free the country from control of the largely foreign-owned mining companies, to develop the economy, and to bring about real political democracy.

The MNR regime acted quickly. Beginning in August 1952 it extended the vote to all adults, legalized the formation of labor unions, and nationalized the major tin-mining companies. A year later, through its land reform law, it broke up the estates of the large landlords and transferred ownership of the small plots to Indian farmers (campesinos). It began extensive projects for education and founded medical clinics in the countryside and farm cooperatives among the peasants. The second MNR president, Hernán Siles Zuazo, came into office in 1956, and Victor Paz was returned to the presidency in 1960.

Prior to 1952 it was barely legal for Indians to attend independent schools. For example, Quakers began missionary work among the Indians in Bolivia in the 1920's, and helped them establish schools beginning in the 1930s, but these first schools had to be clandestine. When the Constitution of 1952 was promulgated the number of Quaker schools quickly multiplied until there were about 50 serving primarily Aymara youth. It was in 1952 that the Indians were first recognized as citizens and began to participate in the political life of their country.

During its years in power (1952-64), the MNR provided Bolivia with the most stable and open government in the country's history. The press was free to criticize the government and did so energetically. Government changes in 1956 and 1960 were the result of elections, although there were frequent crises and many attempts to oust the MNR. Victor Paz Estenssoro's second presidency was ended by a military coup in 1964, and the next eighteen years saw a succession of coups and juntas.

The Second Revolution

There was a second revolution in 1982. In 1980 General Luís García Meza seized power, suspended the constitution, and instituted a repressive regime. His opponents were arrested and killed, and many more fled abroad. The universities were closed. The army ousted García Meza in 1981, and moderate army leadership held power until former MNR president Hernán Siles Zuazo was installed as president by elections held in 1982. Presidential elections in 1985 returned Paz Estenssoro to the presidency. Since 1982, governments in Bolivia have been chosen by election with the participation of a wide range of political parties.

This has however not resulted in proportional power for the indigenous peoples, since political parties and elections require experience and financial resources lacking to the Indian populace. The last MNR president, Gonzalo Sánchez de Lozada, continued strengthening public education, but he is an advocate of capitalism and globalization, policies that conflict not only with dominant interests of the Indians but also with the economic policies of Victor Paz. He served as president from 1993 to 1997 and was re-elected in 2002 but then forced to resign by a popular uprising in 2003. (See "Bolivia in Turmoil," Buffalo Report 17 October 2003, and "Bolivia at a Crossroads" Bolivia at a Crossroads," Buffalo Report 5 December 2003.)

The Growth of Aymara Political Power

The reforms of the MNR in the revolutions of 1952 and 1982 made possible the growth and consolidation of Indian political power that now begins to eclipse the MNR. During the past decade two Indian leaders have become especially prominent, both Aymara. They are Felipe Quispe, known as "El Mallku," a member of Parliament and leader of a significant party whose power base is the Aymara farmers of the Altiplano (especially north of the capital around Achacachi and the towns of Warisata and Pucarani); and Evo Morales, also a member of Parliament and leader of another significant political party, the Movement Toward Socialism (MAS), whose power base is the unions, (particularly the miners and coca growers). Quispe and Morales are often political opponents, particularly when seeking the allegiance of residents of El Alto, the sprawling burgeoning city of 800,000 on the Altiplano just above La Paz, where recent events have revealed a third powerful Indian political force, FEJUVE. What all three have in common is a determination that Indian interest not be swept aside by political and economic policies. There has been an overwhelming support for this common element among the Indians, particularly among the Aymara, even though there has been some questioning of specific demands and specific tactics.

The chief tactic, invented by Quispe, at least in its application to politics in Bolivia, has been roadblocks. These roadblocks are simple low-tech affairs, consisting of rocks across the main highways. The Indians who put up these roadblocks visit the roadblocks on a daily basis and confront soldiers or anyone who attempts to remove them. Quispe initiated roadblocks early in 2003 on the roads north of La Paz, cutting the road from La Paz through Achacachi (an often restless Aymara city on the Altiplano) to Sorata, a center for trekking and other tourism at the foot of Mt. Illampu, northern anchor of the Cordillera Royal. The isolation of Sorata prompted the government to evacuate tourists by means of military helicopters, resulting in a skirmish in which some dozen Indians were killed. These deaths led to increasing Aymara support, including that of Morales, for Quispe's blockades, which deprived the capital city of La Paz of fuel and other supplies. When President Gonzalo Sánchez de Lozaro ordered the military to escort oil trucks into the city on October 12, there was a major clash in the indigenous city of El Alto, resulting in 3 dozen deaths. This action infuriated the whole country, and during the following week half a dozen cities were on strike demanding the resignation of Sánchez, which duly occurred on Friday October 17.

Felipe Quispe had initiated the blockades of 2003 demanding revision of the contracts for exploitation of gas reserves by international consortiums, but what led to the massive protest was the shedding of Indian blood in El Alto. I witnessed marches and demonstrations throughout that week, and on the third and fourth days I felt confident enough to go out and watch from the side of the street, since the marches were well disciplined and entirely peaceful. The insistent demand at the time was for the resignation of the President, and hence the immediate crises was easy to resolve. The underlying crisis did not however disappear.

The Indians have a strong sense of foreigners having repeatedly come to Bolivia to take away their riches and leave them nothing. For two centuries, Bolivia was the main source for Europe's silver and more than 100,000 Indians and Africans died in the rich mines at Potosí, which in the seventeenth century was the largest and richest city in the Americas in spite of being at an altitude of over 15,000 feet. After silver, it was guano, which Chile took along with Bolivia's coastline. And then it was tin. Now that Bolivia has been found to possess the second largest reserve of natural gas in South America, the Indians are determined that this resource not be taken away as in the past, with no benefit to themselves. This determination is without a doubt a result of the awakening that began with the revolution of 1952.

THE DEMANDS OF 2005

The specific demands with which the Bolivian Parliament is confronted at the beginning of June are complex and in part contradictory. There are three specific demands, two of them presented by the Indians of western Bolivia, and one by the entrepreneurs of eastern Bolivia. The two demands from western Bolivia are demands by the Indians that they count for more than they have in the past. One is a demand that the hydrocarbon resources of the country be nationalized, with a view to their exploitation by Bolivia rather than an international consortium. The other is a demand for a Constitutional convention, with a view to increasing and institutionalizing the role of impoverished Indians in the government of Bolivia, and hence also in the determination of policies pertaining to natural gas reserves and other resources. The third demand comes from the entrepreneurial class around the city of Santa Cruz, and it calls for greater autonomy for the departments (states) of Bolivia, with a view to keeping the economic prosperity of Santa Cruz in that area rather than sharing it with the Indians on the Altiplano. Not surprisingly, Quispe, Morales, and FEJUVE are pressing the first two demands and opposing the third.

My involvement with Bolivia over the past six years has been primarily with Bolivian Quakers, nearly all 30,000 of whom are Aymara. I know some Bolivian Quakers who are middle class, including one who is an M.D. and works for USAID on the control of infectious diseases, one who was Undersecretary of Education in a previous government, and some professionals such as teachers and architects. For the professionals an income of six or eight hundred dollars a month is very good. Most of the Quakers I know, and the vast majority in Bolivia, hardly make that amount in a year. I have helped arrange higher education (post-secondary) scholarships for Bolivian Quakers, and their applications more often than not reveal that their parents' income is less than the meager scholarship of fifty dollars per month. Generally, the family home is in the country on the Altiplano with subsistence farming, and the house has no electricity, no heat, no running water, and dirt floors. Vast numbers of these peasants are moving into cities, very often to get a better education and more economic opportunity, but unemployment is widespread, underemployment is virtually universal, and poverty is extreme. This is the background for the Indian demands that are making today's headlines and preparing the way for a third revolution.

There are significant differences between the Indian demands of 2003 and those of 2005. In 2003 there was no realistic prospect that the departure of President Sánchez would result in greater economic well-being or institutional power for the Indians. It was certain that he would be replaced by another member of the elite, as indeed happened. In 2005, the demands are specifically aimed at improving economic well-being and strengthening the institutional power of the Indians. Hence the demands of 2005 are far more difficult to achieve, partly because they involve working out a host of details and partly because the elite (including the new entrepreneurs in Santa Cruz) have more to lose this time. Another difference is that the marches and demonstrations of 2003 were generally nonviolent, and almost completely so after the first day. In 2005, there have been more incidents of violence and more threats of violence. Demonstrators have broken the windshields of busses and taxis that tried to operate during the final days of May and the first days of June, peaceful Aymara marchers were attacked with clubs and stones in Santa Cruz last week, and there have been threats of taking over the Parliament or burning it down. The combination of the vast difficulty of achieving the demands and the increased threat of violence makes the situation in 2005 more ominous than that of 2003, as well as more important for the future of Bolivia.

The demands from eastern Bolivia for more Departmental autonomy (roughly, more States' rights), which are not Indian demands at all, add a complication that is difficult to assess. As with the other demands, the details make a great deal of difference, for autonomy can mean many different things. Furthermore the specific tactics that might be used are uncertain. Altogether missing from the demands so far described are the interests of those in southern Bolivia, around Tarija, where the gas reserves are located and where the populace has benefited economically from the investments of the foreign oil companies. Tarija might be inclined to support the demands for autonomy from Santa Cruz, but so far has not mounted any well-publicized campaign along that line.

RISING TO THE CHALLENGE

The two great needs of Bolivia at the present time are for more power and respect for the native peoples and more economic activity that benefits the whole country. How to integrate those two requirements is and will remain an enormous challenge. Rising to meet that challenge, if such occurs, will constitute the third Bolivian revolution. Like the first two it will have to be a revolution of the left, leading to more power to the Indians, less poverty and oppression, and less exploitation by foreign corporations. It is not likely to be popular in Washington.

The incumbent president, Carlos Mesa (see "The Anti-political Politician: Reflections on Bolivia," Buffalo Report, 26 March 2005), was the running-mate of President Sánchez in 2002 and succeeded to the presidency when Sánchez resigned. His background is an historian and a television journalist. He is thoroughly legitimate, but he lacks ordinary political instincts, has never personally been elected to office, is not a member of any political party, and has so far refused to use armed forces to break up demonstrations, marches, or blockades. Political analysts generally consider him weak, based, I am convinced, on their macho confusion of strength with dominance and their equally macho blindness to the difference between dominance and endurance. Mesa aims at conciliation rather than domination, and he seems determined to serve out his mandate until the presidential elections of 2007.

On June 3 the Catholic Church, at the invitation of President Mesa, offered to facilitate discussions among the contending parties, contingent on the parties putting aside violence and showing respect for one another during the talks, and Mesa set October 16 as the date for both a referendum on autonomy and the election of delegates to a Constitutional convention. These steps further prepare the way for a third revolution to occur in Bolivia, with even less bloodshed than those of 1952 and 1982. But of course dark forces still lurk in the wings.

(6 June 2005)

11 Bolivia: Roadblocks to Power

Questions of Power and Violence

In Bolivia roadblocks are not an obstacle to power but an instrument for attaining and exercising power. During May and June of 2005 mainline newspapers in the US often described the groundswell of opposition in Bolivia as violent demonstrations. On the other hand, when I spoke with Bolivian friends of mine, who are Indians and Quakers and advocates of nonviolence, they generally objected to characterizing the uprising in Bolivia as violent. Our perceptions and our judgments are often heavily influenced by words like "violent", so it might be useful to try to sort out just what is involved with respect to what happened in Bolivia.

Two facts are beyond question. One is that the principal tactic of the demonstrators was a type of blockade, and the other is that very little blood was shed on either side. It is remarkable that so little blood was shed in three weeks of intense demands and demonstrations involving hundreds of thousands of marchers and attempts to take over parliament and the presidential palace. The credit for this remarkable achievement belongs to both parties. The demonstrators had stones and clubs but no firearms. This was undoubtedly known to the police and the army, and reassured them that the officers and soldiers were not in mortal danger during the confrontations. The police and military did, of course, have powerful weapons, but their front line of defense consisted of water cannons, tear gas, and rubber bullets. There was a double cordon of police and military surrounding Plaza Murillo where the parliament and presidential palace are located. The skirmishes which occurred when the militants attempted to take over those symbolic buildings were won by the security forces without loss of life, and without the use of lethal force.

Much credit goes to President Mesa and the security forces for limiting themselves to non-lethal force in securing Plaza Murillo. If Plaza Murillo and its buildings had been occupied by the rebels, or if there had been demonstrators killed by security forces in the skirmishes, the momentum of the confrontation would have swung decisively in the direction of the rebels. After all, it was the deaths that occurred in skirmishes in 2003 that intensified the demands that forced Gonzalo Sánchez from the Presidency in October of that year. In 2005, the authorities had clearly learned their lesson and were determined not to make the mistake that Sánchez had made in 2003.

One death did occur just a day before the resolution of the drama. Unable to meet in Plaza Murillo and hoping for a more tranquil venue, Congress scheduled a meeting hundreds of miles away in Sucre, the official capital of Bolivia. Miners, who had been leaders of the protest from the beginning, sped down to Sucre in trucks, and one of their leaders was killed in a confrontation with the soldiers on the outskirts of town. But the drama was already in its final scene, and the one death did not affect its conclusion. In retrospect, it remains astonishing that three weeks of such intense protests by so many thousands of farmers, teachers, coca-growers, and miners, all Indians, resulted in only one fatality.

Does the absence of fatalities signify that the confrontations were not violent? That is the question with which we began, and we may expect differing answers so long as the question is posed in those terms. My Quaker Indian friends gave an affirmative answer. When I suggested to one that there seemed to be more violence in 2005 than in 2003, he insisted that the protests were not violent affairs. Turning from the action of the protestors and demonstrators, I mentioned that Aymara marchers had been attacked with clubs and stones when they attempted a peaceful march into Santa Cruz. He replied that no one was seriously hurt, and that those using the clubs and stones were in any case a group of right-wing young people opposed to the aims of the demonstrations. I did not pursue with him how he understands the conception of violence, partly because I do not trust my Spanish enough to enter into a discussion that requires careful wording. He did not deny that there was violence and I am inclined to credit him with a conception according to which violence is less violent, and perhaps negligible, if there are no fatal casualties or if it occurs in the course of demonstrating for justice. Recognition of degrees of violence strikes me as a more reasonable posture than an absolute conception according to which an action is definitively either violent or not violent. Such a conception of degrees of violence, although rarely encountered in the public media, is probably the most widespread conception in practice. There will of course be endless disputes about what makes an action more or less violent, but general agreement to distinguish levels and grades of violence makes sense and facilitates reconciliation following a confrontation.

BLOCKADES, ROADBLOCKS, ETC.

That brings us to the question of roadblocks and blockades. The article on blockades in my 1958 edition of the Encyclopedia Britannica explains that a blockade is an act of war implemented by naval forces. The article discusses various legal conditions and qualifications pertaining mostly to the nineteenth and twentieth centuries, but the conception is obviously too narrow for us. In discussions of the protests in Bolivia the phrase "road blockade" has often been used, and this would simply be a contradiction in terms, if the encyclopedia's definition were the whole story. In Bolivia road blockades, or roadblocks, have been a tactic of protest for a quarter century, primarily among the Indians of the Altiplano, and they have grown increasingly powerful and effective. They are a tactic that has nothing naval about them at all, that does not occur in the context of war, and that does not depend on firearms or heavy weapons. These three points distinguish the roadblocks in Bolivia from the naval blockades discussed in the encyclopedia. They also suggest that the roadblocks are not violent, or are less violent. About their being less violent I have no quarrel, but I cannot agree that they are nonviolent.

One aspect of violence toward people is that it deprives them of liberty. It is obvious that when a person is raped or assaulted or murdered, that person's liberty of movement has been severely restricted. In his essay "On Liberty" John Stuart Mill insists that the primary principle of liberty is that all persons should enjoy as much liberty as is compatible with equal liberty for other persons. It is useful to think that there is a presumption of violence where Mill's principle of liberty is not respected. Such a conception of violence is bound to be rejected by those who are determined to mold or control the behavior of others, but it is useful despite being controversial. To the extent that this conception of violence is biased, its bias generally works against governments, and it is on the whole salubrious to hold governments to higher standards of criticism

It is evident that blockades of any kind severely limit the liberty of many people. In the recent blockades in Bolivia, the cities of El Alto and La Paz were shut down. There was no public transportation and private transportation was also curtailed. At the beginning of the protests, public buses continued to operate, but were discontinued after a hundred of them had windows broken by stones from the demonstrators. So the buses were forced off the street, as were taxis and private cars. It is true that no lives were lost and that "lethal force" was never employed. But force was employed, and to my mind the roadblocks and the enforced suspension of transportation constituted a form of violence.

In the United States and in Europe protestors have sometimes engaged in sit-downs at the entrances to facilities to whose work the protestors have had moral objections. These protests, in which people have blocked entrances and have chained themselves to trees or gates, have not involved the same degree of violence as throwing rocks at bus windows. They have generally been characterized by the press and the police as well as by the organizers as non-violent protests. Certainly they have been less violent than the recent protests in Bolivia. In the United States a person arrested and convicted for such an act would not be classified as having been convicted of a violent crime. In Germany however, deliberately sitting down on a driveway so that a truck would have to run over you to enter or leave has been defined in law as an act of violence (*Gewalt*). The point is that such an act violates Mill's principle of liberty, depriving truck drivers of the liberty of entering or exiting without running over a human being. This German legal conception of violence results is a much broader conception of violence than the conception of violence that requires that there be bloodshed or death, though it remains narrower than that of Gandhi or King.

The blockades in Bolivia have been a political rather than a military tactic. This has resulted in their being less violent, but the element of violence should not be overlooked. There must have been civilian deaths in La Paz during the three weeks of demonstrations and protests, and it is likely that some of these deaths (it is midwinter, after all) were hastened by shortages of food and fuel. Blockades like these are a more powerful weapon than boycotts, strikes, and embargos. Boycotts seem a relatively benign form of pressure or economic coercion, causing hardship but not curtailing liberty. Strikes are in principle equally nonviolent, and are included as such in Staughton Lynd's survey of nonviolence in the USA. In practice they have at times become more violent, as when company property has been trashed or scabs beaten up. Embargoes, however, do curtail liberties and they can cause death. The embargos on Iraq from 1991 to 2003 were claimed to be responsible for many thousands of infant deaths. Such embargos violate Mill's principle, since they curtail the liberty of trade, and they do contain an element of violence.

Nothing much should be made of the fact that these Indian roadblocks in Bolivia were part of a political rather than a military campaign, and that the Indian cause has a powerful claim to justice because of centuries of oppression. Clausewitz famously reminded us that war and politics are inseparable, saying that war is a continuation of politics by other means. So politics must also be a version of war, using other means. The common element is the attempt to call the shots, dominate other people. Roadblocks as well as naval blockades can be a means to achieve power and domination, and the Bolivian Indians have been using them effectively. The recent events of 2005, like those of 2003, were designed to demonstrate and expand the power of the Indians. They achieved this goal—but they achieved only this goal, since the substantive issues about the gas reserves, restructuring political authority, and regional autonomy remain unresolved.

Although a pacifist, I am not inclined to criticize the Bolivian Indians who have adopted roadblocks as a political tactic. The poverty and oppression imposed on the Indians for four centuries by the ruling elite from overseas is a flagrant injustice. It is no doubt by necessity rather than free choice that the Indians are now combating this injustice by political rather than by military means. There is, as Robert Mugabe and George Bush have brilliantly demonstrated, no guarantee that power achieved politically will remain benign. Nonetheless, using political means, even where some degree of violence is involved, leaves better chances for a resolution that will not tear the country apart but will instead facilitate greater peace and prosperity. Let us hope that the new interim President, Eduardo Rodríguez, can help the contending parties, who remain fiercely at odds, find such a mutually acceptable path.

Bolivia Now: The Confrontation Still to Come

The events of June replaced one anti-political politician with another. Substantively nothing was accomplished—no relief of dire poverty and no redress of standing injustices. Nor is there a President who can exercise substantive leadership in the manner of Victor Paz Estenssoro. Like Carlos Mesa, Eduardo Rodríguez belongs to no political party, has no political base, and has never been elected to office. That is all to the good, since the political parties are, with the exception of MAS (Movement toward Socialism), rooted in the past and aligned with the interests of the ruling non-Indian elite. Eduardo Rodríguez is an interim president, with limited but unclear powers. His principal mandate is to call for early elections, within six months. This will surely occur. Early elections is one of the four demands of the campesino demonstrators who forced Mesa from office, and is the only one of the four that meets with no opposition, since it is a procedural matter that gores no one's ox. Two of the other three are vital to changing the locus of power in Bolivia, and the fourth aims at retribution against the last elected president, Gonzalo Sánchez de Lozada. In addition there is a demand from right-wing politicians in Santa Cruz (the free-enterprise hub of Bolivia) for regional autonomy.

The three principal campesino demands are for a constituent assembly, for nationalization (again) of the oil and gas reserves in Bolivia, and for the imprisonment of Sánchez de Lozada. The aims and interests behind these demands are for re-alignment of representation in the Senate and the Chamber of Deputies so as to coincide with the population of the country, to prevent foreign interest from exploiting (as they have regularly in the past) the natural resources of Bolivia without any benefit to Bolivian Indians, and to resolve the powerful and persistent anger among Indians about the roughly one hundred fatalities (mostly Indians) during 2003.

President Rodríguez has now decreed that general elections (for senators and deputies as well as for president and vice-president) will be held on December 4, at which time there will also be balloting for the Constituent Assembly. Elections by themselves are unlikely to change to allocation of power significantly. In the election of 2002 Evo Morales, the Aymara leader of MAS, came in second in the balloting. But all three of the top contenders achieved between 21% and 23%, and the traditional elite easily combined forces to deny Morales the presidency. It could happen again. In June of 2005 Morales was one of three announced candidates, who are roughly tied at about 20% in the polls. Curiously, ex-President Mesa, who is ineligible, out-polled them all at 25%. Mesa had vowed to serve out his mandate until the regularly scheduled elections of 2007, so having early elections is a clear achievement of the protests and demonstrations, however those elections turn out.

Natural resources have traditionally been nationalized in Bolivia. The big resource, which lasted for centuries, was silver. The mines at Potosí, a city at an elevation 15,000 feet and 300 years ago the largest and richest city in the Americas, filled Spanish coffers for centuries, and financed the Armada that was destroyed by Queen Elizabeth's navy at the end of the 16th century. There was no thought of privatization in those days. When the silver was exhausted, the same mines produced tin, until the price of tin collapsed. The Indians of Bolivia gained nothing at all from the development of these resources—the benefits and the resources were alike shipped abroad, or retained by those descendants of Europeans who remained resident in Bolivia. There is now a widespread realization of this history and an increasingly sharp determination that it not be repeated. Hence the strident demand for nationalization and the fierce opposition to regional autonomy. (The gas and oil deposits and reserves are located in parts of Bolivia remote from those departments where the Aymara and Quechua predominate, so one clear consequence of regional autonomy would be to limit the benefits these Indians would derive from such resources.) It is difficult to imagine a significant compromise on this issue, even though the prospects for early development and for income from exports thereby become dim. For more than two years the demand of the most prominent Indian politician, Evo Morales, was for 50% control, but he was eclipsed by those calling for 100% control and now seems to have fallen in with that demand.

The demand that Sánchez de Lozada be incarcerated is ominous. It is based on the deaths that occurred in the confrontations in 2003 (see my earlier essays) and attempts to lay the whole blame and responsibility for those deaths on the then president. For such a claim to be valid, the roadblocks would have to have been a wholly legitimate exercise of power and the use of governmental power to end them wholly illegitimate.

Nearly every political theory would conclude the opposite. Civil society is based on government having a monopoly of legitimate coercive force. By claiming that their roadblocks were the only legitimate coercive force, the campesinos were in effect claiming to govern; in other words, they were rebels engaged in a rebellion. All current and recent heads of democratically elected governments would use armed force to suppress rebellion, and none would acknowledge responsibility—regret maybe, but not responsibility—for deaths and injuries that occurred in the ensuing confrontations. There is an arrogance in this campesino demand for vengeance that casts an ominous shadow over future prospects in Bolivia.

Regional autonomy appeals to business groups in Santa Cruz and Tarija, who called for a national referendum on the issue to be held on August 12. Santa Cruz has oil, close ties with Brazil, and thriving businesses. Tarija has the huge gas reserves. The purpose of regional/departmental autonomy is to insulate those rich, or potentially rich, departments from control by the central government, and especially from taxation to assist the development of impoverished areas of the country. It is therefore a move to try to ensure that the richer get richer and the poor stay poor. Though its name may smell like a rose, autonomy in Bolivia therefore has a distinctly dark side. Other parties are willing to have the referendum that is demanded, but not before the elections in December—so certainly not on August 12. President Rodríguez included in his election decree a refusal to order any other balloting before December 4, so the decision on autonomy is postponed, though it is not likely to go away.

The Constituent Assembly is also postponed until after the elections. An Aymara friend of mine writes: "Constituent Assembly means participation of social factions such as miners, campesinos, and other groups that exist in Bolivia, to decide about the political constitution of the Bolivian state." That sounds momentous indeed, like a constitutional convention. The Indians are determined to use it to increase their role in government to roughly their proportion in the population, roughly 65% or 70%, and also to embed in the constitution national ownership and control of all natural resources, water as well as hydrocarbons. There will be intense contrary pressure from Washington, as there was behind the scenes in the recent change of leadership. In view of the politicking to which such gatherings are invariably subject, the outcome is far from secure.

PROSPECTS

The roadblocks have vastly augmented the political power of the peasants and the indigenous people in general. This increased power will probably be confirmed in the elections, but it is unlikely that the peasants and the left will have a clear-cut victory. The three right-wing parties appear likely to agree on a single candidate for the Presidency, which would greatly increase the chance of one candidate (possibly Morales) gaining a majority and thereby winning the election outright. If no candidate wins a majority, which is still the most likely outcome, the election is thrown into the Congress and the leading candidates work out deals in the age-old tradition of back-room politics. The congress in question will be the newly elected congress, which should include more indigenous members, but the ingredients for a deal are bound to be subtle and complex.

There are now three parties representing indigenous people. One is that of Felipe Quispe with its strength among Aymara peasants in the Altiplano. Quispe, known as "El Mallku" (the boss condor), initiated the roadblocks and protests in 2003; he has been largely silent this year, but I expect him to be a significant factor in the elections. The second is MAS, the socialist party of Evo Morales, whose main strength is with the unions (miners, coca-growers, teachers) and in external support from Hugo Chávez and others; MAS has shown more sophistication than Quispe's group in electioneering, in parliamentary coalitions, and in securing media attention. The third group, FEJUVE (Federación de Juntas Vecinales - Federation of Neighborhood Groups), arose in El Alto during the 2003 confrontations and is led by Abel Mamani; its strength is in the city of El Alto, it represents the urbanization of Indian political power, and it undoubtedly profited more through the recent demonstrations than any other group. As peasants continue to move from the country to the city, Mamani may replace Quispe as one of the top two indigenous leaders in Bolivia.

Decisions in Bolivia will be made in the shadow of the G-8 summit at Gleneagles. It is well known that the summit decided to forgive certain foreign debts of the 18 poorest nations, including Bolivia. It is less well-known that the debt relief is conditional upon the nations in questions adopting neo-conservative economic policies, both with respect to macroeconomic stability and also with respect to allowing foreign investments and unrestricted imports. The Bolivian economics minister has already characterized the free trade aspect as unfair because of US agricultural subsidies, foreign investment invariably bleeds resources out of the country (that, after all, is its purpose), and the conditions seems to clash head-on with the determination of indigenous Bolivians to gain control of Bolivia's energy resources. The G-8 is clearly backing the US policy of opening third-world countries to exploitation by international firms. So even with the best imaginable results in the December elections, the future hardly looks rosy.

Bolivia, on the other hand, has as two of its neighbors and trading partners Brazil and Argentina, which are prominently defiant of US trade policies, and the left-leaning indigenous groups in Bolivia can count on support from Hugo Chávez in Venezuela and Fidel Castro in Cuba. With international finance, world trade policies, control of energy supplies, global ideology, and breaking out of poverty and oppression all hanging in the balance, the December elections loom larger than usual on the world scene. In such confrontations it is usually the interests of the impoverished Indians that lose. But in Bolivia the events of 2003 and 2005 have shown that the Indians have now acquired a powerful veto, and there is in any case a leftward momentum in large parts of South America. It will be interesting to watch.

Roadblocks have been the means to power for all three indigenous political groups. Roadblocks, however, are intrinsically negative. They can no more serve as an instrument of government than can the Pentagon troops in Iraq or the bomb at Hiroshima. It remains to be seen whether and in what way the show of overwhelming power to shut things down can transform itself in the upcoming elections, in the new congress, and in the Constituent Assembly.

(12 July 2005)

Epilogue

Heraclitus's Reply

for Franz Jägerstätter

I: Anticipation

> And indeed there will be time to wonder.

"I only know . . . " begins the poet,
The words, confirming each in his prison,
Turn once in my door and turn once only.
Their Ariel sound bestows a brief caress,
Foreplay, I devoutly hope, for my unprisoning,
And I grow tense, as, to that end,
The body of meaning follows on, testing
The skeptical anfractuosities that wall me in.

"*I* only know . . ." -?
Does he think himself Prometheus, revealing
Secrets somehow stolen from the gods,
That would save humanity, or damn it,
If once released from quintessential privacy?

What precious daedal gift of knowledge
To transmute the data of experience
To universal truth that will compel
Each stranger as it compels oneself!
I have no way to bring myself to doubt
The joys and pains that trill my blood --
Nor words, alas, to bring that certainty to others.
Knowing's distant cousin to such unbending mind,
Shared through common access to the facts,
And constrains belief in proportion to its proof,
Which is not proof if hidden from our view.

Datum. Given. Gift. Giftig.
Sharing the unshared inmost things,
This gift is plainly an illusion.

           "I *only* know . . ." -?
Is this some rock-bottom bedrock
Once-in-a-lifetime revelation,
Truth that is blindness in the early afternoon
As the midwinter sun flames the ice and snow
And holds that one moment's light alone?
What blessing of great comfort
To thus defy our ever-changing world
Of never-isolated facts! The ordinary picture
With which we model and confront reality,
Though it must have its parts, contains
No elements so fixed in their invariance,
Nor, aping wholes, so wholly on their own.
Light dawns gradually over the whole
With unexpected interplay of sun and shade
Which seems more giving than given, settling
Like a house whose own foundation walls
Are held up by its joists and roof,
To accommodate recalcitrant experience.

           "I only *know* . . ." -?
Does the poet, then, disclaim belief,
Compelled by unrelenting logic
To acknowledge abstract truth
From which his heart withholds assent,
Parched, watered, and unable to drink?

What solace dearly purchased,
To cleave the soul's dominion
And banish reason off to Avignon!
Aporetic Callicles, akratic lush,
Unbeliever keeping still a place set

For a long-lost murdered son --
Such people thwart rebuttal and consent.
Deep the need and deeper still the moat,
High the risks and higher still the wall.
But limits of language limit our world.
The peace of mind that these defenses guard,
Past the deep moat and the high wall,
Sequestered in the inmost secret room,
Lies beyond the reach of human talk,
Outside our ken.

The search for criteria, for touchstones of meaning
And of knowledge, is a search for community,
In which we strive to gather one another in.
I fear the dark exclusions of the poet's start
Cannot release the tumblers of the lock
Which holds the two of us apart.

II: ENCOUNTER

                    We had the experience but missed the meaning.

". . . that he who forms a tie is lost."
What's this? Do you withdraw the key?
Did you then not speak to me?
Are your words -- and mine --
Private grumblings accidentally overheard,
Never meant to breach the prison yard?

III: REPOSE

                                  . . . but the agony abides.

". . . that he who forms a tie is lost.
The germ of corruption has entered his soul"

Truth that is half-truth, half-truth that is error,
For the way up is the same as the way down.

Paolo and Francesca, seeking
A little love in a cold world, forming
A bond that shut the world out, circling
Forever like a foetus in search of a womb,
Are eternally entwined in eternal isolation,
Dry, unwatered, uprooted from the whole.

The way up and the way down are the same.

Uprooted, too, the poet-hero, holding
Himself aloof from attachments, knowing
The corruption of a carnal tie, preparing
To stand naked and alone before his God
    ("I was thirsty, and ye gave me no drink.")
Proud in a forgetful bravery, thinking
    ("I was a stranger, and ye took me not in.")
To find in heaven what he disdained on earth.

The way down and the way up are the same.

We cannot share the moment on the cross,
The April bullet on a Memphis afternoon,
Nor lesser woes that each is called to bear.
Actions, too, devolve on each of us alone:
Conforming steps harmonious with a crowd
Through riot or rule or military stride,
Are reckoned nil in the summation of a soul,
Unless, by waste, they negative the whole.
The poet knows, as I know too,
That he who needs the solace of a mate,
Not just for laughter and rejuvenation,
But to put aside the grounds of blame and praise
And ride with him the tumbril to his fate,

LIMITS TO POWER

Turning this his finest human blessing
Into a crutch to bear the weight of action,
Has lost the nerve to see the whole thing through,
Deceiving us his stranger-friends, me and you,
Who could have, would have, been his soul's mates.
In Caesar's realm, where all that matters
Is neatly circumscribed in space and time
And has a value pegged by markets and alliances,
One must often stand or fall alone
Thereby to bind a multitude of ties
That will support one's soul.

Knower who is unknowing
Sharing that is unshared
Bonds that set us free
"Yes" that signals self-denial
"No" that thunders affirmation
Love that always and never changes:
The way in and the way out
The way forward and the way back
The way up and the way down
Are one and the same.

NOTES:

The story of Franz Jägerstätter, beheaded in Berlin on August 9, 1943, is told by Gordon Zahn in *In Solitary Witness*. There is now a stained glass window to him in the Votivkirche in Vienna.

Leslie Fiedler also thundered "No!"

Graham Greene used Conrad's lines (from *Victory*) as epigraph for *The Human Factor*.

The refrain in Part III is a fragment from Heraclitus which T. S. Eliot used as epigraph for "Burnt Norton" and in the text of "The Dry Salvages."

The aporeia of Callicles occurs in the latter part of Plato's *Gorgias,* Steph. 481ff— e.g., 481c, 497a-b, 505c, 513c.

On "akratic lush," see Book VII of the *Nicomachean Ethics,* where Aristotle discusses *akrasia* (incontinence), a state in which persons abstractly know what needs to be done but their actions suggest that they do not really believe what they know.

Dante tells the story of Paolo and Francesca in Canto 5 of his *Inferno.*

Besides obvious borrowings from T. S. Eliot (including all the epigraphs), Part I contains numerous phrases, and some whole lines, drawn from F. H. Bradley, L. Wittgenstein, W. v. O. Quine, J.-P. Sartre, and S. Cavell.

APPENDIX:

"Heraclitus's Reply" is the most obscure thing I have ever written. It is an Eliot take-off. I have always had lines from Eliot banging around in my head, but this piece would never have been written if I had not co-taught a seminar on Eliot with Lionel Abel during his final semester at UB. It is written with an admittedly mischievous delight in pedantic references, challenging vocabulary, monstrously long sentences (like Gjertrud Schnackenberg), the tri-lingual pun, and juxtaposition of classical and contemporary images. I am in particular impishly pleased with the sentence lifted verbatim from Bradley's *Appearance and Reality,* "This gift is plainly an illusion," which no colleague in philosophy has been able to identify after being told that one line is from Bradley.

I am, of course, dead serious as well as impishly pedantic. Knowledge is both essentially social and intrinsically coercive: nothing personal counts as science, and what matters is not who knows it but rather that it is known; and then anyone who rejects or disputes what is known is (perhaps politely, but still firmly) excluded from further dialogue, as creationists have no voice in biology and Velikovsky and his students have no voice in cosmology. So what is essentially private or secret can only fraudulently be claimed as knowledge, as seems done by Conrad. In this context Wittgenstein's remark, "'Knowledge' and 'certainty' belong to different categories," has largely unexploited critical potential in political discussion. — I am not sure just what to say discursively about this matter, any more than about the matter of forming ties, which is surely a road to salvation as well as to perdition; so I have tried this form of expression, limping along toward a quasi-mystical resolution with the crutch borrowed from Heraclitus. (Heraclitus offers us philosophers only crutches, not solid staffs such as those of Kant, Frege, Wittgenstein, or the Pragmatists.)

The envoi at the end of Part I is from Stanley Cavell, whose skepticism is more anfractuous than mine, though he might not use that word. Both Stanley and I have written extensively about Wittgenstein's conception of criteria. I have here used lines from his *The Claim of Reason*, where he departs subtly but definitively from Wittgenstein by supposing that we must search for criteria. (Wittgenstein regarded them as embedded in the language-games that are part of our human natural history.) Since the search is hopeless, there being no criterion for success, this move entrenches Stanley's skepticism.

I have added notes about the most arcane matters. I assume that readers can find the Eliot if they wish, and which lines come from the various philosophers does not matter that much, however annoyed some of their epigones might be at my rash amalgamation of Quine and Wittgenstein. (There are lines from both Quine and Wittgenstein in the same sentence at the end of the second skeptical anfractuosity.) The line "Sequestered in the inmost secret room" echoes Jean-Paul Sartre's play, *Les sequestrés d'Altona*. I should probably add for readers under forty that Martin Luther King, Jr., was assassinated in Memphis on April 4 (Good Friday, as it happened), 1968.

I remain unhappy about the obscurity of the reference implicit in the line, "Which is not proof if hidden from our view," which targets the Pentagon-CIA-White House secrecy as well as the bulging briefcase of Senator Joe McCarthy; but I don't see how to make that explicit without destroying the tone of the poem. All the other obscurity is deliberate.

(1 March 2004)

CENTER WORKING PAPERS

Newton Garver: *Limits of Power: Some Friendly Reminders.* 2006.

John Henry Schlegel: "Like Crabs in a Barrel: Economy, History and Redevelopment in Buffalo." 2005. *

Bruce Jackson: *Late Friends.* 2005

Diane Christian and Bruce Jackson, *The Buffalo Film Seminars, Series I-X Spring 2000—Spring 2005.* 2005

Diane Christian: *Blood Sacrifice.* 2004. .

Koichi Suwabe: *A Faulkner Bibliography.* 2004.

Dianne Hagaman: *Howie Feeds Me.* 2004.*

William Benzon: Chicago's "Millennium Park." 2004*

Emile de Antonio in Buffalo. 2003.

Bruce Jackson: *The Peace Bridge, Chronicles.* 2003.

(*Asterisked items are available for free download at the CWP website: http://centerworkingpapers.com.)

FORTHCOMING

Jerry L. Thompson: *Coney Island 1973* [2006]

Robert Creeley: *Poets Work* [2006]

Leslie A. Fiedler: *Starting in Newark* [2006]

William R. Greiner and Thomas E. Headrick, with W.J. Snyder, *Location, Location, Location: A Special History of the University of/at Buffalo.* [2006].